LearningPlus®

Self-Paced Learning of Skills and Strategies

An Innovative
Instructional
Handbook
for Building
Reading Skills

Reading

More than 300 pages of instruction and practice in how to read and locate information.

 ETS™ Educational Testing Service

Contents

How to Use This Handbook

The LearningPlus® Reading Handbook will help you learn and apply the reading skills you will need to succeed in college and in the workplace. You can use this handbook for guidance and additional practice as you complete the LearningPlus Reading Course. You can also use this handbook as an independent study guide to supplement other mathematics courses or activities.

The LearningPlus Reading Handbook offers a lively, realistic approach to reading. Examples and comments from successful readers in real-world settings will help you become a better reader.

Here is what you will learn in each chapter.

LearningPlus

LearningPlus is a computer-based instructional program available at many institutions. For more information about this course, refer to the insert included in this handbook.

Chapter 1: Understanding Ideas	This chapter helps you become better at finding the main idea of a paragraph or article and comprehending what you read.
Chapter 2: Answering Questions	This chapter helps you develop strategies for answering literal questions and questions that may require you to make an inference about what you read.
Chapter 3: Evaluating Ideas	This chapter helps you learn how to evaluate ideas as you read to decide whether the author provides good arguments and sufficient evidence to support his or her position.
Chapter 4: Researching Ideas	This chapter helps you learn how to compare and contrast information you gather from different sources.
Chapter 5: Locating Information	This chapter helps you learn how to read and interpret different kinds of resources, including charts, graphs, maps, and other reference sources.

To use the LearningPlus Reading Handbook effectively, follow the steps listed below.

1. Follow the numbers.

Like many handbooks, this book uses numbers to refer to chapters, sections, and subsections. For example, 3.1 refers to chapter 3, section 1. The chapters and sections are arranged in a logical sequence so you can progress from one to the next. There are also times when it makes sense to quickly refer back or ahead to other sections. When this happens, you will find the numbers useful to locate these sections.

2. Read the instruction and examples.

Each section of this handbook contains a lesson. The lesson explains a concept or skill, then shows examples. Read this information carefully before checking your understanding.

3. Refer to definitions and related topics.

Watch for definitions of critical terms in the margins. You can also look up definitions in the glossary or find terms listed in the index at the end of this handbook. In addition, some sections list topics that are related to the section. Refer to these related handbook sections for review or further information.

4. Check your understanding.

You'll find a set of questions at the end of almost every handbook section. Answer these questions to see how well you understand the explanations and examples.

5. Look up the answers and explanations.

After you answer each set of questions, look in the *Answers to Questions* section at the end of the chapter. This section not only shows the answers, but also provides explanations that will help you understand the concepts better.

To locate the answers to a particular set of questions, look for the number listed above the questions. This number is the same as the section number, except that it may be followed by an *a* or *b* if there is more than one set of problems in the handbook section.

For example, if you finish the questions for section 3.1 and wish to check your answers, look under *Answers to 3.1* in the *Answers to Questions* section at the end of Chapter 3.

Understanding Ideas

Learn how to improve your
reading comprehension.

1.1 Skimming

Skimming an article gives you a sense of what it is about and how it is organized.

You can use what you learn from skimming to:

- Decide whether you want to read an entire article or book.
- Make **predictions** about an article before reading it.

When you skim first, you know what to expect from an article and are therefore more prepared to read it. Skimming helps you focus on an article's important ideas and improves your ability to understand what you read.

These are the parts of an article that are generally most useful to skim. Refer to the numbered labels on the following article to see examples.

1 ▷ title

Titles sometimes state the topic of an article or its most important idea. For example, this title lets you know that the article is about choosing a smoke detector.

2 ▷ first paragraph

First paragraphs sometimes contain the most important idea of the article. This paragraph says that people should install smoke detectors in their homes.

3 ▷ last paragraph

Sometimes the last paragraph reemphasizes the important ideas contained in the article. This paragraph restates the most important idea of this article: that people should install smoke detection systems in their homes.

4 ▷ headings

Headings are often centered or appear in bold type. The headings in this article describe types of smoke detectors, for example, an ionization smoke detector.

5 ▷ first sentence of each paragraph

The first sentence of each paragraph lets you know that the paragraph describes a type of smoke detector. The first sentence of a paragraph sometimes gives the topic that the whole paragraph will discuss.

⑥ **words in special type**

The word *slower* stands out because it is in italics. Sometimes words in special type give you information about an article's topic or organization. At other times, bold or italic type is simply used to emphasize a word or phrase. This is the case with the word *slower*.

The article below shows the parts that are usually most useful to skim. (Lines are used to represent the rest of the text in the article.)

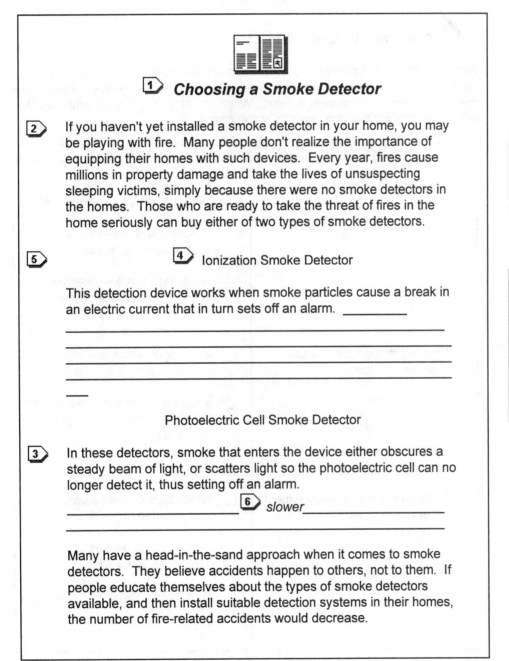

① ***Choosing a Smoke Detector***

② If you haven't yet installed a smoke detector in your home, you may be playing with fire. Many people don't realize the importance of equipping their homes with such devices. Every year, fires cause millions in property damage and take the lives of unsuspecting sleeping victims, simply because there were no smoke detectors in the homes. Those who are ready to take the threat of fires in the home seriously can buy either of two types of smoke detectors.

⑤ ④ Ionization Smoke Detector

This detection device works when smoke particles cause a break in an electric current that in turn sets off an alarm. _____

Photoelectric Cell Smoke Detector

③ In these detectors, smoke that enters the device either obscures a steady beam of light, or scatters light so the photoelectric cell can no longer detect it, thus setting off an alarm.

⑥ *slower*

Many have a head-in-the-sand approach when it comes to smoke detectors. They believe accidents happen to others, not to them. If people educate themselves about the types of smoke detectors available, and then install suitable detection systems in their homes, the number of fire-related accidents would decrease.

first sentence of each paragraph

The first sentence of a paragraph sometimes gives the topic that the whole paragraph will discuss.

words in special type

The word *slower* stands out because it is in italics. Sometimes words in special type give you information about an article's topic or organization. At other times, bold or italic type is simply used to emphasize a word or phrase. This is the case with the word *slower*.

After skimming the preceding article, use what you've learned to answer the questions below.

▶ **Tip:** Remember, the parts of an article that are generally useful to skim, such as the first and last paragraphs and first sentence of each paragraph, are *most likely* to let you know what the article is about. If these parts don't contain the information you need, try skimming a little more. For example, if the first paragraph doesn't give you an idea of what the article is about, read the second paragraph.

✓ **Check Your Understanding 1.1**

See if you can answer these questions based on the parts of the "Choosing a Smoke Detector" article shown on the previous page. Put a check (✓) next to the correct answers in the answer column. When you finish, look at the entire article in the *Answers to Questions* section of this chapter.

Question	Answer
1. This article is most probably about	____ choosing a smoke-detection system for the fire department. ____ choosing a smoke-detection system for your home. ____ choosing a smoke-detection system for your workplace.
2. What information is this article most likely to contain?	____ information about the types of smoke-detection systems ____ statistics showing the number of U.S. offices using each type of smoke detector
3. Which question would you expect this article to answer?	____ Which type of smoke detector was invented first? ____ How do the two types of smoke detectors compare? ____ How do you install a smoke detector?

1.2 Predicting

Every time you read, you make guesses about what's coming next. Usually, you don't pay much attention to the guesses you are making inside your head. When you use **predicting** as a reading strategy, you *deliberately* make guesses — or predictions — about what you are reading.

Predicting helps you in several ways to understand what you are reading.

Look at the comments of the people below to learn why they make predictions.

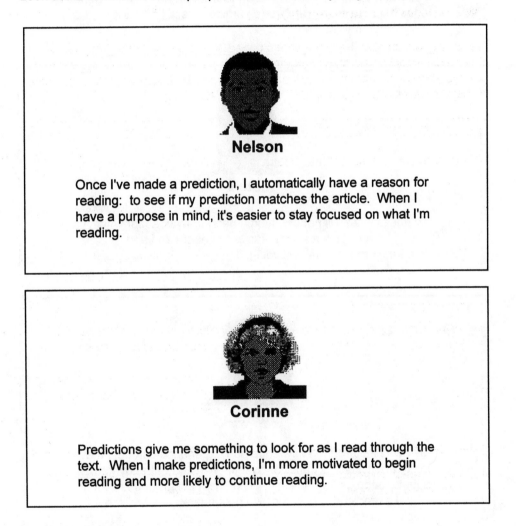

Nelson

Once I've made a prediction, I automatically have a reason for reading: to see if my prediction matches the article. When I have a purpose in mind, it's easier to stay focused on what I'm reading.

Corinne

Predictions give me something to look for as I read through the text. When I make predictions, I'm more motivated to begin reading and more likely to continue reading.

Tai

Predictions help me pay attention to what I read. I can't figure out if my prediction matches the article unless I'm paying attention to my reading.

Latiya

To guess what will happen next, I need to think about what I've already read. This makes it easier to understand and remember the ideas I'm reading.

Alonso

My own background knowledge and experience can help me make predictions. I can ask myself, "What do I already know about the topic of an article?" Using my background knowledge to make predictions can improve my understanding of the article I'm reading.

▶ **Tip:** It doesn't really matter whether your predictions are accurate. What's important is that predictions give you a way to measure what you are reading.

✓ **Check Your Understanding 1.2**

Read the paragraph below and then answer the following questions.

How much sleep do you need each night in order to feel refreshed the next day? The amount of sleep that people need seems to vary from individual to individual. Some people are long sleepers and others short sleepers. The long sleepers are those that need about 10 hours of sleep a night. . .

Put a check (✓) next to the correct answers in the answer column. When you finish, refer to the *Answers to Questions* section to see the entire paragraph.

Question	Answer
1. Based on what you have read so far, guess what the next part of the paragraph will be about.	____ how shift workers cope with changes in sleep patterns ____ the amount of sleep that short sleepers need ____ the effect of jet lag on sleeping patterns
2. Which quote from the paragraph helped you predict the next part?	____ "The amount of sleep people need each night seems to vary..." ____ "How much sleep do you need each night...?" ____ "Some people are long sleepers and others short sleepers."
3. What other information could the next part of the paragraph contain?	____ more information about the amount of sleep people need ____ information about when people dream ____ information about what kinds of sleep medication work best

1.3 Questioning

creating questions

Questioning means asking yourself (or fellow students) questions about what you are reading in order to practice finding the important ideas in texts. For example, if you wanted to know if someone understood a paragraph about cloud creation, you might ask them how clouds are formed.

To make sure you understand what you are reading, try making up a question about what you have read. **Creating questions** as you read improves your understanding by forcing you to think carefully about what you've read.

Read the comments of the people below to learn more about creating good questions.

Hamid

I begin by looking for the most important idea in the paragraph. This is the main message that the text expresses. I think to myself, "What is this paragraph about?" If it's about how a car engine works, I might ask, "How does burning gas in an engine make the wheels of the car go around?" Someone would have to understand the paragraph about a car engine to answer that question.

Yuma

I always remember to focus on the big picture and avoid detail questions. Detail questions usually won't check a reader's understanding of the most important idea. In general, I try to avoid questions that can be answered with a simple *yes* or *no* or a one-word answer.

▶ **Tip:** Creating questions is also a great study tool, especially if you write down the answers to your questions. When you're finished reading, you will have a list of questions and answers that get at the most important ideas from the article. You can read them to review for an exam instead of going through the entire article again.

✓ Check Your Understanding 1.3

Refer to the paragraph below to answer the questions that follow.

You hear them everywhere, on TV, in conversations at work, among teenagers, words like: "buzz off," "lighten up," "geek," "grub," and "moola." These expressions may sound like a foreign language, but they're not. They're just slang, words on the changing edge of our language. Many of these slang terms originate within subcultures of our society. Occupational groups such as truck drivers, police, and medical personnel create their own slang. Teenagers, sports groups, and the movies are examples of other sources in society that contribute to the creation of slang. For example, most people first heard the expression "ten grand," meaning $10,000, from the movies. This term, along with slang terms from many other groups, has now been adopted by society in everyday conversation.

Put a check (✓) next to the correct answers in the answer column.

Question	Answer
1. What is the most important idea in this paragraph? (What is the paragraph about?)	____ There are many examples of how slang is used all around us. ____ Slang terms are heard everywhere in our society. ____ Many slang terms come from the subcultures in our society.
2. Which question would you ask to see if someone understood the paragraph above?	____ What are some slang words used in our culture? ____ Where do many slang words come from? ____ What does the slang term "ten grand" mean?
3. On the subject of slang in general, which of the following is a big-picture question?	____ What is an example of a slang term used in sports? ____ How does slang affect the development of language? ____ Has society become more tolerant of slang?

1.4 Clarifying

All readers come across articles or sections of articles that are difficult to understand. The important thing is to notice when you are getting confused and then do something about it.

There are several tactics you can use to **clarify** difficult or confusing parts of an article.

Read the comments of the people below to learn about different ways to clarify what you read.

clarify

Clarifying means figuring out the meaning of confusing words, sentences, or sections in an article.

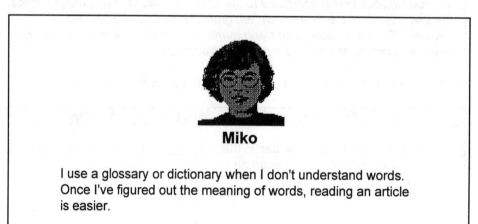

Miko

I use a glossary or dictionary when I don't understand words. Once I've figured out the meaning of words, reading an article is easier.

Hamid

When pieces of writing are particularly complicated or difficult, it helps me to read them more than once. Rereading is also helpful if I've been reading too quickly or not paying close attention.

Yuma

When I come to a difficult section of an article, I try looking ahead to see if there will be more information later. Authors often introduce complex ideas and then explain them later on. Notice how the second sentence below explains the first.

Neither found the logomachy enjoyable. Arguing over which word to use in their slogan seemed to be a waste of time to them both.

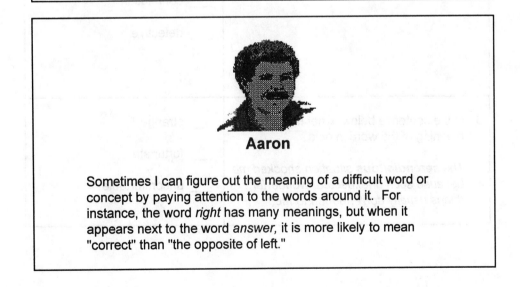

Aaron

Sometimes I can figure out the meaning of a difficult word or concept by paying attention to the words around it. For instance, the word *right* has many meanings, but when it appears next to the word *answer,* it is more likely to mean "correct" than "the opposite of left."

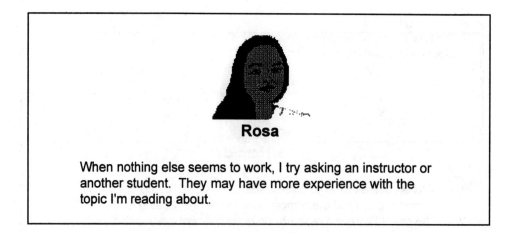

Rosa

When nothing else seems to work, I try asking an instructor or another student. They may have more experience with the topic I'm reading about.

 Check Your Understanding 1.4a

Put a check (✓) next to the correct answers in the answer column.

Question	Answer
1. In the sentence below, what is the meaning of the word in bold? *It was obvious to the detective that the information was not **pertinent** to the case, but his assistant kept trying to establish a connection.*	___ related ___ useless ___ interested in
2. What word in the sentence helps you clarify the meaning of *pertinent*?	___ information ___ connection ___ detective
3. In the sentence below, what is the meaning of the word in bold? *The **serendipitous** situation shocked me because such unexpected, wonderful things usually don't happen to me.*	___ strange ___ fortunate ___ uncomfortable

4. What word in the sentence helps you clarify the meaning of *serendipitous*?	___ situation ___ happen ___ wonderful

 Check Your Understanding 1.4b

Refer to the paragraph below to answer the following questions.

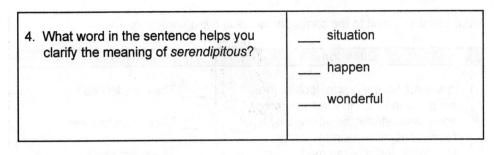

Ad Appeal

Advertising is big business, as companies scramble to capture new and bigger markets in an increasingly competitive economy. To sell their products, most companies still rely on basic appeals that have proved effective over time. These appeals include the lure of a more comfortable life, greater enjoyment, improved appearance, a healthier body, having a secure retirement, more money, better employment, and increased popularity. When an advertiser sells a product using these appeals, the emphasis is on the benefits that come to the buyer, not on the product itself. So, for instance, if you see a fitness machine advertised in the newspaper, you're likely to read more about how the machine will give you a "meaner, leaner" figure than how the machine actually works.

In addition to relying on the basic appeals, advertisers are always searching for new, more effective advertising strategies. Advertisers face very few limitations in their quest for new ways to entice the consumer to buy. **Advertising strategies are constrained only by minimal laws, self-imposed industry standards, the limits of the media, and the creativity of advertising agencies.** Recent trends in advertising include repetition, bombarding a target audience with ads in every form of media possible. Another popular strategy is using price appeals, such as "buy one and get a second one free" or "pay no interest." Price appeals are probably used more frequently and successfully than any other appeal. You simply have to open a newspaper or turn on the TV to see the latest version of this popular appeal.

Put a check (✓) next to the correct answers in the answer column.

Question	Answer
1. In the *Ad Appeal* article, look at the sentence in bold. In what way are advertising strategies affected by legal restrictions, advertising industry standards, limits of the media, and creativity?	___ They are limited. ___ They are improved. ___ There are more strategies.
2. Which sentence helped you clarify the meaning of the sentence in bold?	___ In addition to relying on the basic appeals, advertisers are always searching for new, more effective advertising strategies. ___ When an advertiser sells a product, the emphasis is on the benefits that come to the buyer, not on the product itself. ___ Advertisers face very few limitations in their quest for new ways to entice the consumer to buy.

1.5 Summarizing

1.5.1 Including Important Ideas

Summarizing a piece of writing increases your understanding by making you decide what ideas are most important. When you summarize, your main goal is to state clearly and briefly the **most important idea** from your reading.

Read each person's comments to learn how they find the most important idea in their reading.

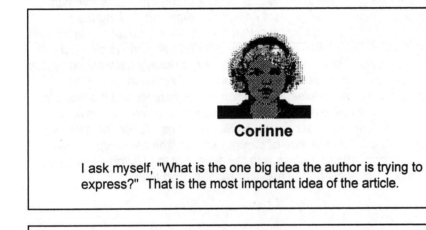

Corinne

I ask myself, "What is the one big idea the author is trying to express?" That is the most important idea of the article.

Tai

I ask myself, "If someone asked me to give him or her a quick overview of what this is about, what would I say?" This helps me find the most important idea.

▶ **Tip:** Sometimes a piece of writing will contain its own summary. When you are asked to "summarize" or "find a summary statement," try looking for a sentence or paragraph that briefly states what the text is all about. When a piece of writing *doesn't* contain its own summary, you need to read all of the ideas and then state the most important message in your own words.

---

summarizing

Summarizing is a strategy in which you restate what you've read in a shortened form, keeping only the most important ideas. You can summarize any piece of writing: a sentence, a paragraph, a section of text, an article, or an entire book.

most important idea

The most important idea is the main message that a piece of writing expresses — the one idea that ties together all of the ideas you have read. The most important idea is sometimes called the main point or main idea.

 **Check Your Understanding 1.5.1**

Look for the most important idea in the following paragraph. Then answer the questions that follow.

When Benjamin Franklin suggested the idea of saving daylight in a whimsical essay he wrote in 1784, he probably never imagined that his wishful thinking would be enacted into law by the U.S. Congress, but it was. The Uniform Time Act, passed in 1966, established a uniform system of daylight-saving time throughout the United States. In most states, moving the clocks ahead an hour in the spring results in an additional hour of daylight in the evening. Many people are happy to have more daylight so they can prolong their outdoor evening activities. Others feel that having an extra hour of daylight in the evenings gives them a psychological boost. Not everyone is pleased with the system, however. Farmers' work schedules are usually determined by sun time, not clock time. As a result, the change to a new system during the summer disrupts their schedules. In addition, many parents find it difficult to persuade young children to go to bed at the usual time when they have to compete with the extra hour of light during the evenings. Since the days when people first started taking the idea of daylight-saving time seriously, it has been a controversial subject. Even with the advent of the Uniform Time Act, not everybody is uniformly happy about daylight-saving time.

Read the paragraph on the previous page to answer the questions below.
Put a check (✓) next to the correct answers in the answer column.

Question	Answer
1. What is the most important idea in this paragraph?	____ People like to have extra daylight during the summer months. ____ Farmers don't like switching from one system to another. ____ People have differing views about the benefits of daylight-saving time.
2. How do you know this is the most important idea in this paragraph?	____ The most important idea is never stated, but the other ideas back it up. ____ The most important idea is stated at the beginning of the paragraph. ____ The most important idea is stated several times in the paragraph using different words.

1.5.2 Dealing with Details

A **summary** should contain details that help you (or someone else) understand the most important idea from your reading. A **detail** is a specific piece of information on any topic. Because details often deal with particular small bits of information, they are considered less important than larger ideas.

summary

A summary is a shortened version of a piece of writing that contains its most important ideas. You can summarize any piece of writing: a sentence, a paragraph, a section of text, an article, or an entire book.

Read the comments of each person below to learn more about dealing with **details**.

Nelson

Sometimes authors include information that is not closely related to their main topic. At other times, they include examples, quotes, and statistics that don't relate directly to the main message. None of these details should be included.

Latiya

I don't list items such as "milk, canned salmon, broccoli, and blackstrap molasses" individually in my summaries. If I need to mention these items, I try to sum them up in a short phrase such as "foods that contain calcium."

Alonso

Instead of including every detail, I create a general statement that describes how the details relate to the main message of the text. Here's an example: An article may discuss five different studies on the subject of pets. Instead of mentioning every study, I could substitute a general idea that describes their results, such as "studies show that having a pet can improve a lonely person's health."

✓ **Check Your Understanding 1.5.2**

Read the paragraph below and answer the questions that follow.

You've heard all the warnings about keeping in shape in order to have a healthy heart. So, you've decided to start a fitness program. But what makes up a good fitness program for keeping your heart healthy? Many people would simply start by choosing an activity, any activity, such as swimming, jogging, bowling, tennis, baseball, basketball, walking, cycling, golf, volleyball, or horseshoes. Not just any activity will do, however. To choose activities that will have the best fitness benefits for your heart, you need to select ones that exercise the large muscles of the body, are rhythmical, and don't involve long periods of rest. Activities such as swimming, jogging, walking, and cycling meet these requirements. They are called aerobic activities. Once you select an aerobic activity for your fitness program, you should plan each exercise period to last a minimum of 20 minutes with the heart beating at a moderate level. Doing the right kind of exercise for the right amount of time is an essential part of a good fitness program. Finally, the most critical feature of a good fitness program for the heart is sticking with the program. It takes consistency over time for an aerobic fitness program to have a training effect on the heart
-- creating a healthier, more efficient heart .

Put a check (✓) next to the correct answers in the answer column.

Question	Answer
1. Which is the best short description for swimming, jogging, walking, and cycling?	____ irregular activities ____ small-muscle activities ____ aerobic activities
2. Which is the best short description of the effect of a good fitness program on the heart?	____ causes a training effect on the heart ____ The heart beats at a moderate level for a minimum of 60 minutes. ____ continuous rapid beating of the heart

3. Which of these is the best summary of this paragraph?

____ When planning a fitness program for the heart, choose activities such as walking, cycling, jogging, or swimming that will have a training effect on the heart.

____ When planning a fitness program for the heart, choose aerobic activities that have a training effect on the heart. Also, make sure each exercise period lasts at least 20 minutes; and plan to exercise consistently over time.

1.5.3 Writing Summaries

Sometimes you will want to take the **summarizing** strategy one step further by actually writing a summary. Summaries contain the most important information from the book, article, or paragraph that they describe.

Summaries make great study tools. Writing a summary helps you think about the important ideas from an article, and reading over your summary helps you remember those ideas later.

▶ When you write a summary:

- Find the most important ideas and any ideas needed to explain them.
- Condense those ideas into a sentence or two for a short article, or a paragraph or two for a longer article.

summarizing

Summarizing is a strategy in which you restate what you've read in a shortened form, keeping only the most important ideas. You can summarize any piece of writing: a sentence, a paragraph, a section of text, an article, or an entire book.

Latiya

As I read, I highlight some of the words, phrases, and sentences that seem to be most important. After I finish reading, I look back over this information and ask myself: "How are all these ideas related?" I try to answer that question in my summary buy using some of the important words and key ideas I highlighted.

Read the paragraph below and answer the following questions.

Since the mid-1970s, the modern office has become increasingly computerized. Microprocessors, small chips that perform the central processing tasks at the heart of the computer, are found everywhere. Familiar office equipment, such as calculators, telephone systems, facsimile (FAX) machines, photocopiers, typewriters, and dictation machines now have these tiny chips built into them. Microprocessors make all these machines more efficient and "intelligent" — capable of adapting more readily to the needs of the user. In fact, the microprocessor has not only improved many of these machines, it may be making some of them obsolete. Computers, which also use microprocessors, are taking over many tasks that used to require separate machines, such as word processing, voice mail, telecommunications, and FAX transmission. All these changes brought about by the microprocessor have made office operations easier and more efficient.

 Check Your Understanding 1.5.3

Put a check (✓) next to the correct answers in the answer column.

Question	Answer
1. A summary of this paragraph should	____ mention the names of modern office equipment. ____ mention the impact of the microprocessor in the office. ____ mention the importance of FAX machines.
2. Which of these is a better summary of this paragraph?	____ **Summary 1** The microprocessor has revolutionized the modern office and is used in most office equipment, including computers. This processor has speeded up office operations and made them easier. ____ **Summary 2** The microprocessor is now used in calculators, telephone systems, FAX machines, typewriters, dictation machines, and computers.

1.6 Answers to Questions

Answers to 1.1

Here is all the text for the article "Choosing a Smoke Detector."

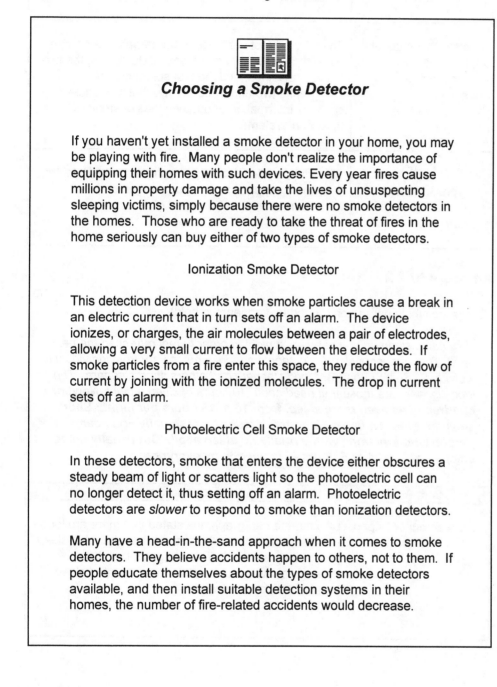

Choosing a Smoke Detector

If you haven't yet installed a smoke detector in your home, you may be playing with fire. Many people don't realize the importance of equipping their homes with such devices. Every year fires cause millions in property damage and take the lives of unsuspecting sleeping victims, simply because there were no smoke detectors in the homes. Those who are ready to take the threat of fires in the home seriously can buy either of two types of smoke detectors.

Ionization Smoke Detector

This detection device works when smoke particles cause a break in an electric current that in turn sets off an alarm. The device ionizes, or charges, the air molecules between a pair of electrodes, allowing a very small current to flow between the electrodes. If smoke particles from a fire enter this space, they reduce the flow of current by joining with the ionized molecules. The drop in current sets off an alarm.

Photoelectric Cell Smoke Detector

In these detectors, smoke that enters the device either obscures a steady beam of light or scatters light so the photoelectric cell can no longer detect it, thus setting off an alarm. Photoelectric detectors are *slower* to respond to smoke than ionization detectors.

Many have a head-in-the-sand approach when it comes to smoke detectors. They believe accidents happen to others, not to them. If people educate themselves about the types of smoke detectors available, and then install suitable detection systems in their homes, the number of fire-related accidents would decrease.

Correct Answer	Explanation
1. choosing a smoke-detection system for your home	The title and first paragraph let you know that the article is about choosing a smoke-detection system for your home.
2. information about the types of smoke-detection systems	The title, the last sentence in paragraph one ("...can buy either of two types of smoke detectors."), the two section headings, and the first sentences of paragraphs two and three tell you that the article contains information about the types of smoke-detection systems.
3. How do the two types of smoke detectors compare?	Since this article is about choosing a smoke detector, you would expect it to give you more information about comparing the two types of detectors.

Answers to 1.2

Here is the whole paragraph (added text appears in bold).

How much sleep do you need each night in order to feel refreshed the next day? The amount of sleep that people need seems to vary from individual to individual. Some people are long sleepers and others short sleepers. The long sleepers are those that need about 10 hours of sleep a night. **Newborn children need even more sleep, from 16 to 18 hours per night. Short sleepers function fine on 5 hours or less. Occasionally you hear of a person who functions with virtually no sleep at all. But usually some sleep — at least 4 or 5 hours — is needed by everyone.**

Correct Answer	Explanation
1. the amount of sleep that short sleepers need	So far, the paragraph has stated that there are long and short sleepers. It mentions the amount of sleep long sleepers need. This suggests that the paragraph will go on to state the amount of sleep that short sleepers need.

2. "Some people are long sleepers and others short sleepers."	This quote tells you that there are long and short sleepers. You can predict that the paragraph will go on to explain the difference between these two types of sleepers. Since long sleepers are mentioned in the next sentence, but short sleepers have not yet been mentioned, you would expect that they might be discussed next.
3. more information about the amount of sleep people need	It makes sense that the information in the paragraph would be about the amount of sleep, rather than dreams or sleep medication.

Answers to 1.3

1. Many slang terms come from the subcultures in our society.	The main idea is the main message that a piece of writing expresses — the one idea that ties together all the ideas you have read. The main idea discussed in this paragraph has to do with the origins of slang words from subcultures in our society. This sentence in the paragraph best captures this idea: *Many of these slang terms tend to originate within subcultures of our society.*
2. Where do many slang words come from?	This question will check a reader's understanding of the paragraph's main message.
3. How does slang affect the development of language?	A big-picture question helps the reader understand the main idea of a piece of writing. "How does slang affect the development of language?" is a big-picture question. The other questions are detail questions. Detail questions usually won't check a reader's understanding of the most important idea because they can usually be answered with a simple *yes* or *no* or a one-word answer.

Answers to 1.4a

Correct Answer	Explanation
1. related	The word *pertinent* means having a clear relation to the matter at hand. You could substitute *related* in the sentence and the sentence would retain its original meaning. ... the information was not **related** to the case...
2. connection	The word *connection* gives you a clue about the meaning of *pertinent*. *Connection* also means being related. It's useful to notice that the sentence contrasts the detective with his assistant. The detective thought the information was <u>not</u> pertinent (related) while the assistant thought the information was connected (related) to the case.
3. fortunate	The word *serendipitous* is used to describe a fortunate accident.
4. wonderful	You know if the situation made the person feel wonderful, then *serendipitous* probably means a fortunate happening.

Answers to 1.4b

Correct Answer	Explanation
1. They are limited.	The sentence in bold means that advertising strategies are limited only by minimal laws, advertising-industry standards, the limits of the media, and the creativity used by advertising agencies.
2. Advertisers face very few limitations in their quest for new ways to entice the consumer to buy.	This sentence precedes the sentence in bold. It says that advertisers face few limitations as they look for new advertising strategies. This gives you a clue that the next sentence will probably list the limits that advertisers face.

Answers to 1.5.1

Correct Answer	Explanation
1. People have differing views about the benefits of daylight-saving time.	The most important idea in this paragraph is that people have differing views about the benefits of daylight-saving time. Reasons are given why some people favor the system and why some people oppose it.
2. This idea is stated several times in the paragraph using different words.	There are a few key sentences that state this most important idea using different words: *However, not everyone is pleased with the system.* *Since the days when people first started taking the idea of daylight-saving time seriously, it has been a controversial subject. Even with the advent of the Uniform Time Act, not everybody is uniformly happy about daylight-saving time.*

Answers to 1.5.2

Correct Answer	Explanation
1. aerobic activities	*Aerobic activities* is the best short description for activities like swimming, jogging, walking, and cycling, which exercise the heart.
2. causes a training effect	The phrase *causes a training effect* is the best short description of the effect of aerobic activities on the heart.
3. When planning a fitness program for the heart, choose aerobic activities that have a training effect on the heart. Also, make sure each exercise period lasts at least 20 minutes; and plan to exercise consistently over time.	This summary tells you the most important ideas of the paragraph. The other paragraph gives unnecessary details and fails to mention several key points.

Answers to 1.5.3

Correct Answer	Explanation
1. mention the impact of the microprocessor in the office.	It is a good idea to mention the impact of the microprocessor in the office. This is the paragraph's most important idea — and you should always include the most important idea in your summary.
2. **Summary 1** The microprocessor has revolutionized the modern office and is used in most office equipment, including computers. This processor has speeded up office operations and made them easier.	This summary is better because it mentions the most important ideas from the paragraph. It explains how the microprocessor has affected office operations.

Answering Questions

Learn skills that will help you answer
questions about the material
you read.

previewing

Previewing means looking at something in advance. For example, when you see previews of an upcoming movie, you look at parts of it to get an idea of what the whole thing is about.

2.1 Previewing Questions

There are times when you know you are going to be asked to answer a set of questions about an article, such as when you are answering questions for a reading assignment or taking a test. **Previewing** the questions before you read an article can make it easier to answer the questions later. If you know what you are going to be asked, you can look for the answers as you read.

▶ To preview questions, follow these steps:

- Read over each question.
- Look for words that give you a hint about what to look for as you read.
- Mark these words in the question, if possible.
- Think about the topics you should keep in mind while reading.

Read the following comments of each person to learn more about the steps for previewing questions.

Latiya

Sometimes I preview the questions by reading each one carefully. At other times, I just glance through the questions to get an idea of what topics to look for as I read. It depends on how much time I have.

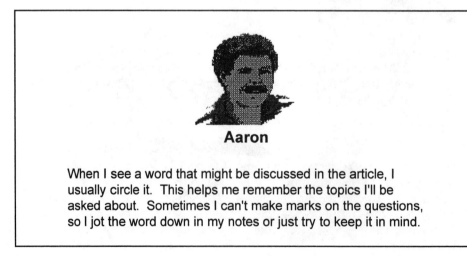

Aaron

When I see a word that might be discussed in the article, I usually circle it. This helps me remember the topics I'll be asked about. Sometimes I can't make marks on the questions, so I jot the word down in my notes or just try to keep it in mind.

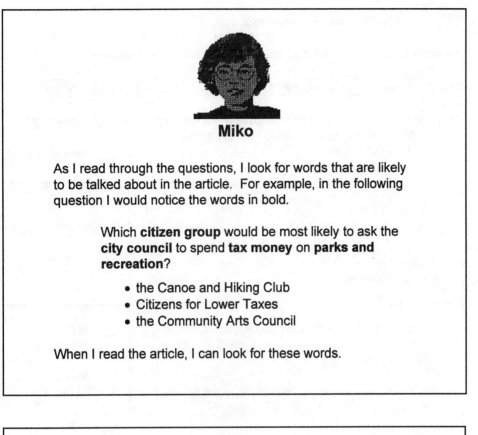

Miko

As I read through the questions, I look for words that are likely to be talked about in the article. For example, in the following question I would notice the words in bold.

> Which **citizen group** would be most likely to ask the **city council** to spend **tax money** on **parks and recreation**?
>
> - the Canoe and Hiking Club
> - Citizens for Lower Taxes
> - the Community Arts Council

When I read the article, I can look for these words.

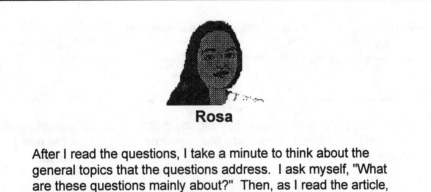

Rosa

After I read the questions, I take a minute to think about the general topics that the questions address. I ask myself, "What are these questions mainly about?" Then, as I read the article, I keep these topics in mind. This helps me focus my reading, and it gives me an idea of what to look for while I read.

▶ **Tip:** When you are reading the article, you won't always remember the words from the questions. That's fine. The point is to keep general ideas from the questions in the back of your mind as you read. If you notice some of the words from the questions, great. Mark them in the passage or jot them down in your notes. If you don't notice any of the words, don't be concerned. You can always go back to the article after you've read the questions again.

Check Your Understanding 2.1

Put a check (✓) next to the correct answers in the answer column.

Question	Answer
1. Read the question and then choose the underlined words you would look for while reading an article. (Mark all that apply.) *According* to the article, which of the following is *mostly lacking* in the *American diet*? • fat • fiber • protein • carbohydrates	___ according ___ mostly lacking ___ American diet
2. Read the question and then choose the underlined words you would look for while reading an article. (Mark all that apply.) *What are two advantages of the new food labels that are on all packaged and canned foods?* • They catch your attention. • They include fat, cholesterol, and sodium content. • They have a nice design. • They include fiber content.	___ two advantages ___ new food labels ___ foods
3. Based on your preview, which **two** topics do you think the article that accompanies the questions above will address?	___ advantages of the new food labels ___ rising number of nutrition-related jobs ___ need for certain types of foods or nutrients in the diet ___ benefits of being a dietitian

2.2 Drawing on Background Knowledge

When you begin to read an article or book, you aren't really starting fresh. You bring into your reading all the knowledge and experience you've gained from the books and articles you've already read, the ideas you've already learned about, and the things you've done during your life.

Drawing on your background knowledge makes it easier to answer questions by helping you:

- Guess where answers will appear in an article.
- **Fill in the blanks** in an author's writing.

Read the following comments of each person to see how drawing on background knowledge can help answer questions.

Corinne

I've read a lot of articles in my life, so I have a pretty good idea about how most of them work. This knowledge sometimes helps me answer questions. For example, if I were reading an article about space travel, I might be asked: "What do scientists predict for the future of space travel?"

Instead of looking at the beginning of the article, I'd probably look near the end, because so many articles are set up to discuss the past, then the present, then the future.

---

drawing on your background knowledge

Drawing on your background knowledge means thinking about what you already know and then applying it to the questions you're being asked. First, ask yourself, "What do I know about this topic?" Then ask, "How do my own ideas and experience apply to this question?"

fill in the blanks

When authors write about a topic, they don't include every single detail. For example, an American author who wants to write about a certain breed of dog will not always say: "Dogs are four-legged mammals. They are a lot like wolves or foxes, except that dogs have adapted to living and working with humans."

Instead, the author would assume that most people know what a dog is and probably have some experience with dogs. He or she would just describe the particular dog and let you fill in the blanks with your own knowledge of dogs.

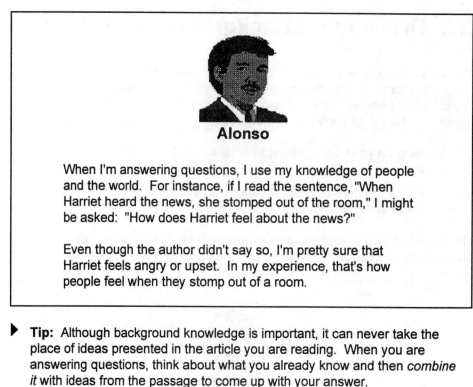

Alonso

When I'm answering questions, I use my knowledge of people and the world. For instance, if I read the sentence, "When Harriet heard the news, she stomped out of the room," I might be asked: "How does Harriet feel about the news?"

Even though the author didn't say so, I'm pretty sure that Harriet feels angry or upset. In my experience, that's how people feel when they stomp out of a room.

▶ **Tip:** Although background knowledge is important, it can never take the place of ideas presented in the article you are reading. When you are answering questions, think about what you already know and then *combine it* with ideas from the passage to come up with your answer.

 Check Your Understanding 2.2

Read the paragraph and questions below. Then answer the questions in the box.

In the early part of this century, George Washington Carver, an agricultural researcher, popularized the use of an obscure plant — the peanut — that originated in the jungles of South America. Carver not only encouraged and helped southern farmers cultivate this plant, but he also developed several hundred industrial uses for peanuts. Recently, researchers in many countries are studying another plant from the tropics that promises to be as versatile and useful as the peanut. In its native India, the tropical neem tree is known as the "village pharmacy." The leaves and seeds of this tree contain substances that kill bacteria and viruses; and neem tea is believed to be a successful treatment for ulcers. Oil from the neem may stop stored apples from spoiling as quickly. In addition, neem powder appears to be an effective natural fungicide and pesticide. The neem tree is not only versatile, but it is accessible as well. It grows quickly and does well in poor soils. These two remarkable plants, the neem tree and the peanut, are examples of botanical treasures from the tropics. It makes you wonder what other miracle plants are waiting to be discovered in some tropical rain forest.

Question 1: What do the neem tree and peanut have in common?

- They are both cultivated extensively by southern farmers.
- They are both used as natural fungicides and pesticides.
- They are both from the tropics and provide many useful products.

Question 2: Why is it significant that the neem tree grows in poor soil?

- It's easy to grow neem trees, so more people can benefit from them.
- It's possible to get oil from the neem tree to protect apples from spoiling.
- The neem tree may provide a new means of producing tea.

Question 3: What idea from the paragraph could be used as a reason for trying to preserve tropical rain forests?

- We can grow more peanuts and neem trees there.
- We have more trees on the earth.
- We can save other plants that might benefit humans.

Put a check (✓) next to the correct answers in the answer column.

Question	Answer
1. To answer question 1 above, it would be helpful to have background knowledge about	____ how to grow plants. ____ how plants are used for different purposes. ____ how to use fungicides and pesticides.
2. To answer question 2 above, it would be helpful to have background knowledge about	____ the climates of tropical areas. ____ bacteria and viruses. ____ what it takes to grow plants successfully.
3. To answer question 3 above, it would be helpful to have background knowledge about	____ the results of destroying tropical rain forests. ____ the conditions in tropical rain forests. ____ where tropical rain forests are found.

2.3 Locating Answers

One way of answering questions is to locate the answer in the article or book you are reading. Sometimes, the wording of a question lets you know the answer is probably in the text.

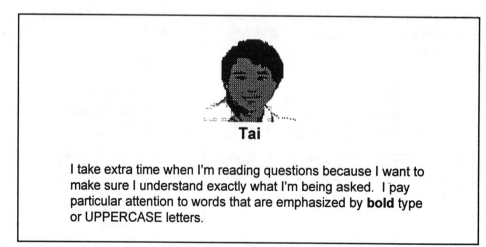

✎ *Example*

Here are some examples:

- *The author states.*
- *According to paragraph 2.*
- *Click on (or circle, or mark) your answer in the article.*

All of these examples point you toward the article itself. When you see this kind of wording in a question, it's a good idea to begin by looking for the answer in the text.

▶ To locate answers in an article, try these steps:

- Read the question carefully.
- Identify words that tell you what to look for in the article.
- Look in the article for these words.
- Use your knowledge of the article to find the answer.

Read the following comments to see how these steps can help you locate answers.

Tai

I take extra time when I'm reading questions because I want to make sure I understand exactly what I'm being asked. I pay particular attention to words that are emphasized by **bold** type or UPPERCASE letters.

Latiya

Most of the time, a question will contain words that tell me what to look for in the article. Here's an example: In the following question, the words in bold tell me to look for a section of the article that talks about the writer's life during the 1970s, or a section that talks about the first National Black Political Convention.

> Which of the following works by Imamu Baraka helped lead to the **first National Black Political Convention** in **1972**?
>
> - *African Congress: A Documentary of the First Modern Pan-African Congress*
> - "Black Nationalist Agenda"
> - *Yugen*

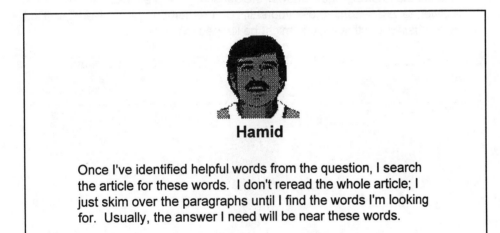

Hamid

Once I've identified helpful words from the question, I search the article for these words. I don't reread the whole article; I just skim over the paragraphs until I find the words I'm looking for. Usually, the answer I need will be near these words.

Yuma

When I'm trying to find an answer, I use my knowledge of the article to narrow my search. For instance, an article about peanut butter might be organized into three sections: where it comes from, how it is made today, and what its nutritional value is. If I am asked what role George Washington Carver played in the invention of peanut butter, I won't look just anywhere for an answer. I'll look in the section that tells where peanut butter comes from.

By noticing the way an article is set up, I can figure out the best place to look for answers.

▶ **Tip:** Sometimes you will know the answer to a question because you remember reading it in the article. When that's the case, don't worry about locating the answer — just answer the question. Before looking for an answer, take a second to ask yourself, "Do I remember the answer?" or "Do I remember where this answer might be located in the article?"

 **Check Your Understanding 2.3**

Read the article below and then answer the questions that follow.

Adult Education is Booming

The number of adults enrolled in educational programs has increased dramatically over the past few years. In fact, adult education is the fastest-growing segment of education, and has been since the 1970s. In 1985, approximately 40 percent of students enrolled in credit courses nationwide were older than 25. During the 1990s, it is projected that adult part-time students will become the majority population enrolled in educational programs.

So why are so many adults returning to school? One reason is corporate downsizing. In lean economic times, corporations try to preserve their profits by combining and eliminating jobs. As a result, many middle managers and other highly skilled employees are being laid off. A good portion of these people are finding it necessary to retrain in order to find new jobs in the fast-changing, competitive economy. In addition, many manufacturing jobs are also changing or becoming obsolete due to new production methods and technology. For instance, many high-paying jobs in heavy industry, such as steel or auto manufacturing, are being phased out completely. These two trends have sent more and more adults back to school.

Even those who haven't been forced out of the work force and required to start another career have found it necessary to extend their education or retrain. The work environment is changing so rapidly that new training is critical. Many companies and professional associations now offer educational opportunities to their employees to help them keep up-to-date on technical and other advances in the workplace. For instance, even five or 10 years ago only specialized people in companies were familiar with computers. Now, nearly every employee must know how to use a computer in some way.

Before 1970, most people preparing for a career planned to prepare only once. Now the exception — preparing for multiple careers during a lifetime — has become the rule. Whether adults are forced to return to the classroom as result of corporate downsizing, of being replaced by new technology and methods, or in order to keep updated in the job they already have, the end result is the same — this country is in the middle of an adult-education boom.

Put a check (✓) next to the correct answers in the answer column.

Question	Answer
1. Which words in this question let you know what to look for in the article? *Which sentence shows one reason more adults are enrolling in educational programs?*	___ "...one reason adults are enrolling" ___ "...educational programs?"
2. Which of the following would help you locate the answer to this question? *Which sentence shows one reason more adults are enrolling in educational programs?*	___ rereading the first and last paragraphs ___ skimming through the article to see where reasons are mentioned or the word *reason* is used ___ noticing how the title relates to the rest of the article
3. Which words in this question give you a clue that the answer is probably in the text of the article? *The author states that the nature of many manufacturing jobs is also changing. Why is that?*	___ "The author states..." ___ "...manufacturing jobs..." ___ "also changing."
4. Suppose you remember that the author organized the article by giving three answers to this question: *So why are so many adults returning to school?* Under which of the author's reasons listed here would you expect to find the answer to the following question? *The author states that the nature of many manufacturing jobs is also changing. Why is that?*	___ because of corporate downsizing ___ because new production methods and technology are making jobs obsolete ___ because many must retrain to keep their current jobs

2.4 Inferring Answers

Sometimes the answer to a question isn't directly stated in the article. You have to figure out what the article implies — what it *indirectly* suggests. This is called making an **inference** or inferring an answer.

The words in a question can often let you know that you'll need to make an inference.

✏️ *Example*

Here are some examples:

- *What does the author assume?*
- *What does the article suggest?*
- *Which of the following can be inferred?*
- *What do you think?*

Each of these examples suggests that you need to think *beyond* the explicit wording of the passage: You need to read between the lines or consult your own opinions. When you see this kind of wording in a question, you should be prepared to make an inference.

▶ To infer the answer to a question, try these steps:

- Read the question carefully.
- Look for words that can help you make an inference.
- Search the article for useful information.
- Use your relevant knowledge and experience.

Read the comments of the people below to see how they go through the steps of making an inference.

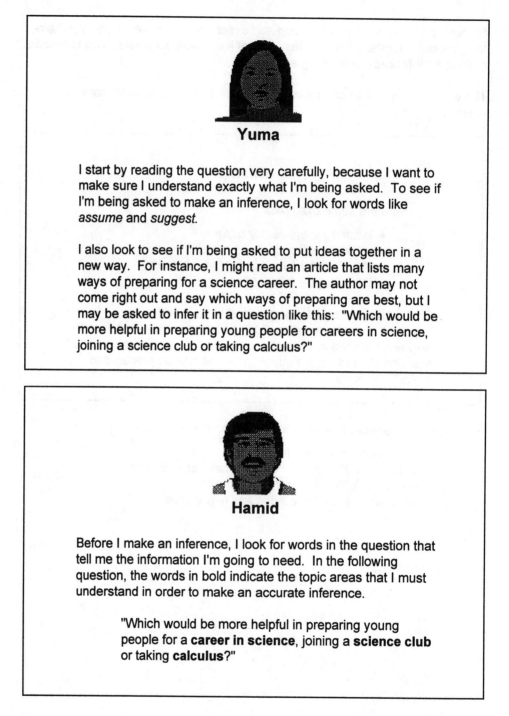

Yuma

I start by reading the question very carefully, because I want to make sure I understand exactly what I'm being asked. To see if I'm being asked to make an inference, I look for words like *assume* and *suggest*.

I also look to see if I'm being asked to put ideas together in a new way. For instance, I might read an article that lists many ways of preparing for a science career. The author may not come right out and say which ways of preparing are best, but I may be asked to infer it in a question like this: "Which would be more helpful in preparing young people for careers in science, joining a science club or taking calculus?"

Hamid

Before I make an inference, I look for words in the question that tell me the information I'm going to need. In the following question, the words in bold indicate the topic areas that I must understand in order to make an accurate inference.

"Which would be more helpful in preparing young people for a **career in science**, joining a **science club** or taking **calculus**?"

Aaron

After I know what topic areas I need to understand, I look for information in the article. If I were asked, "Which would be more helpful in preparing young people for a career in science, joining a science club or taking calculus?" I would look in the article for the words *science, career, club,* and *calculus.*

I would also look for information about organizations, about the importance of socializing with other science-minded people, and about the skills a would-be scientist needs, such as lab experience and knowledge of calculus, physics, and so on. Information from the article is the main ingredient for making an inference.

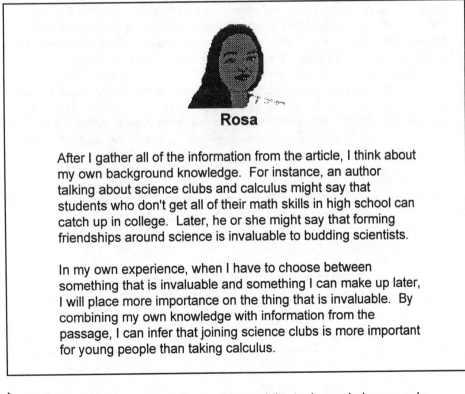

Rosa

After I gather all of the information from the article, I think about my own background knowledge. For instance, an author talking about science clubs and calculus might say that students who don't get all of their math skills in high school can catch up in college. Later, he or she might say that forming friendships around science is invaluable to budding scientists.

In my own experience, when I have to choose between something that is invaluable and something I can make up later, I will place more importance on the thing that is invaluable. By combining my own knowledge with information from the passage, I can infer that joining science clubs is more important for young people than taking calculus.

▶ **Tip:** Knowing the author's feelings toward the topic can help you make inferences. As you read a text, look for words that reveal the author's underlying attitude.

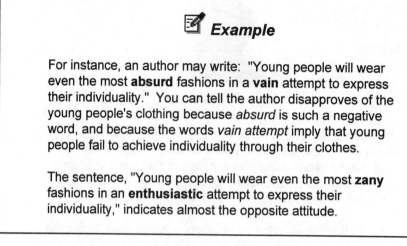

Example

For instance, an author may write: "Young people will wear even the most **absurd** fashions in a **vain** attempt to express their individuality." You can tell the author disapproves of the young people's clothing because *absurd* is such a negative word, and because the words *vain attempt* imply that young people fail to achieve individuality through their clothes.

The sentence, "Young people will wear even the most **zany** fashions in an **enthusiastic** attempt to express their individuality," indicates almost the opposite attitude.

 **Check Your Understanding 2.4**

Read the following paragraph and then answer the questions that follow.

We have become a society that seems unable to function without the credit card. It is such a convenient yet potentially dangerous little piece of plastic. Whether at a gas station, in a store, in a restaurant, or at the theater, many people just whip out a wallet full of credit cards and select one to pay for the goods or services they just received. It's so easy — and somehow, paying with plastic gives the illusion that there isn't the same hole in your wallet that paying with cash produces. Maybe the hole isn't there initially, but eventually it's the same size, or bigger if you have to pay interest. Developing a buy-now-and-pay-later mentality is dangerous, as many Americans who don't control their spending discover when they end up in debt and burdened with huge interest payments.

Put a check (✓) next to the correct answers in the answer column.

Question	Answer
1. What does the author of this paragraph imply when he describes a credit card as "such a convenient yet potentially dangerous little piece of plastic?"	___ Credit cards are better than cash in every way because they are so convenient. ___ There are drawbacks to credit cards when they are not used in a controlled way. ___ Credit cards are convenient, but would be less dangerous if they weren't made of plastic.
2. Which word in the question below tells you that the question requires an inference? *What does the author of this paragraph imply when he describes a credit cards as "such a convenient yet potentially dangerous little piece of plastic?"*	___ author ___ imply ___ describes
3. What **two** pieces of information from the passage could help you make a correct inference for this question? *What does the author of this paragraph imply when he describes a credit card as "such a convenient yet potentially dangerous little piece of plastic?"*	___ the idea that credit cards are so easy and convenient to use ___ the statement that people who don't control their spending end up in debt and burdened with huge interest payments ___ the statement that we have become a society that can't function without the credit card

Topics Related to: Inferring Answers

3.3 Identifying Underlying Assumptions

eliminating

Eliminating answers means deciding that they aren't correct and then ignoring them or even crossing them out, when possible.

2.5 Eliminating Answers

If you can't figure out the correct answer to a question, try **eliminating** the answers that are definitely incorrect.

Read each person's comments to learn how she eliminates answers.

Miko

If I don't remember reading anything about an answer option, I'll cross it out and look more closely at my other choices.

Latiya

When I'm answering questions, I disregard answer options that contain inaccurate information or that don't address the idea the question is asking about.

✓ Check Your Understanding 2.5

Read the paragraph below and answer the questions on the following page.

Who would have thought that the cats, dogs, rabbits, and other furry friends at Ann's pet shop would become regular and popular visitors to the Dennington Care Center? These trips started out as a one-time promotional visit to stimulate Ann's ailing business. But after just one visit, the residents of the care center fell in love with Ann's animals. Ann was amazed at the reception her pets received and vowed to return. And return she did. The animals now come in for three afternoons a week so that the residents can pet them and enjoy their company. Workers in the care center report a noticeable effect on the residents. Some residents who were once depressed and silent now seem livelier and more ready to strike up conversations. Other residents have become more calm and approachable. All in all, Ann, the care center management and residents, and even the pets seem very pleased with the arrangement.

Now answer the following questions without looking back at the paragraph. Try relying on your memory of the paragraph and eliminating unreasonable answers and see how well you do.

Put a check (✓) next to the correct answers in the answer column.

Question	Answer
1. *How often do the animals come into the home?*	____ four times a year ____ three afternoons a week ____ when it's raining
2. *Who enjoys having the pets around?*	____ children ____ teenagers ____ residents
3. *What effect do the pets have?*	____ They make some residents more lively and calm others. ____ They frighten the residents. ____ They annoy the mailman.
4. *Who reports the effect of the pets on the residents?*	____ the local police officer ____ the attending doctor ____ workers in the center

2.6 Summarizing

Many of the questions you face require you to **summarize** a paragraph, article, or section of text. Sometimes the wording of a question makes it obvious that you are being asked to summarize, but sometimes it doesn't.

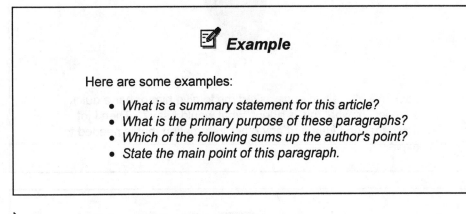

✐ *Example*

Here are some examples:

- *What is a summary statement for this article?*
- *What is the primary purpose of these paragraphs?*
- *Which of the following sums up the author's point?*
- *State the main point of this paragraph.*

▶ To summarize a section of text:

- Find the **most important idea** from your reading.
- Include information that is needed to explain this idea.
- Eliminate unnecessary details.

Sometimes a piece of writing will contain its own summary. When you are asked to "summarize" or "find a summary statement," try looking for a sentence or paragraph that briefly states what the text is all about. When a piece of writing *doesn't* contain its own summary, you need to read all the ideas and then state the most important message in your own words.

summarize

Summarizing means restating in a shortened form what you've read, keeping only the most important ideas. You can summarize any piece of writing: a sentence, a paragraph, a section of text, an article, or an entire book.

most important idea

The most important idea is the main message that a piece of writing expresses — the one idea that ties together all of the ideas you have read. The most important idea is sometimes called the main point or main idea.

Look at the following comments to see how these individuals summarize text.

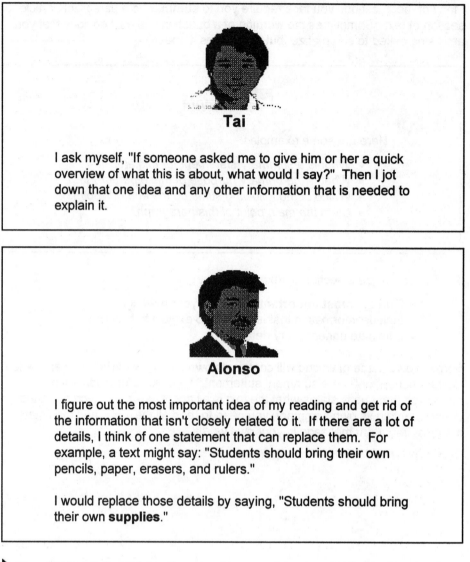

Tai

I ask myself, "If someone asked me to give him or her a quick overview of what this is about, what would I say?" Then I jot down that one idea and any other information that is needed to explain it.

Alonso

I figure out the most important idea of my reading and get rid of the information that isn't closely related to it. If there are a lot of details, I think of one statement that can replace them. For example, a text might say: "Students should bring their own pencils, paper, erasers, and rulers."

I would replace those details by saying, "Students should bring their own **supplies**."

▶ **Tip:** More detailed information about summarizing is provided in Chapter 1, section 5 of the Handbook.

✓ Check Your Understanding 2.6

Read the paragraph below and answer the following questions.

We all thought the answering machine gave us greater control over incoming phone calls, but this control has just been improved. As a phone owner, you can now purchase a display unit that shows the name and phone number of the person who is calling before you pick up the phone. This offers many advantages. First, it allows you to decide if you want to take the call. If you pick up the phone, you can address the person by name as you answer. Second, this system discourages prank phone calls, because you can tell the caller that you know where he or she is calling from. Third, you can keep track of your children. When they call, you know where they are calling from. Another feature of this display unit is that it tells you the name and number of a person who calls and doesn't leave a message on your answering machine. Now you can really surprise these reluctant callers by calling them back to see what they want!

Put a check (✓) next to the correct answers in the answer column.

Question	Answer
1. Which words in the question below tell you that you are being asked to summarize? *What is the main point the author is trying to convey in this paragraph?*	____ this paragraph ____ main point ____ the author
2. A summary of this paragraph should	____ say that control over incoming phone calls has been further improved. ____ give examples of the benefits of the display unit. ____ mention that the display unit provides a good way to keep track of your children.

3. Which of these is a better summary of this paragraph?

Summary 1
Phone-number display units give phone owners more control over incoming calls by allowing them to see the name and phone number of the person calling.

Summary 2
The new phone-number display unit allows you to surprise your neighbors who don't leave messages on your answering machine, because you can get their names and phone numbers from the display unit and call them back anyway.

___ **Summary 1**

___ **Summary 2**

Topics Related to: Summarizing

   1.5 Summarizing

2.7 Answers to Questions

Answers to 2.1

Correct Answer	Explanation
1. mostly lacking American diet	The words *mostly lacking* and *American diet* tell you that you should look for parts of the article that are about nutrients lacking in the American diet. You could look for the words *mostly lacking* in the article or for words that are similar, such as *missing* and *small amounts.* You should also look for the words *American diet* or for similar words.
2. two advantages new food labels	The words *two advantages* and *new food labels* tell you to look for advantages of the new food labels. As you read, you can look for these words or other words that mean the same thing.
3. advantages of the new food labels need for certain types of foods or nutrients in the diet	The first question suggests that the article will say something about the advantages of the new food labels. The second question suggests that the article will discuss the need for certain types of foods or nutrients in the diet.

Answers to 2.2

Correct Answer	Explanation
1. how plants are used for different purposes.	This is helpful background knowledge. If you know how plants can be used for different purposes, you can better understand one commonality between the peanut and the neem tree -- how they can both be used to make many useful products.
2. what it takes to grow plants successfully.	This is helpful background knowledge. Understanding what it takes to grow plants may give you a hint as to why poor soil was mentioned in this article. You may see that if people don't have to worry as much about where they plant the tree, or if they don't have to use fertilizer, then more people may be able to cultivate and benefit from the neem tree.

3. the results of destroying tropical rain forests.	This is helpful background knowledge. If you already know some of the reasons for saving tropical rain forests, it would make it easier for you to understand what this question is asking.

Answers to 2.3

1. "...one reason adults are enrolling"	The words *one reason adults are enrolling* will be most useful in helping you narrow your search for the answer to the question.
2. skimming through the article to see where reasons are mentioned or the word *reason* is used	The article is likely to mention the word *reason* or *reasons*. If you find these words, your answer is probably nearby.
3. "The author states..."	The words *the author states* tell you that the answer is found in the article.
4. because new production methods and technology are making jobs obsolete	Because you know that manufacturing jobs might be related to production methods, you should look in the part of the paragraph where this answer was given.

Answers to 2.4

Correct Answer	Explanation
1. There are drawbacks to credit cards when they are not used in a controlled way.	The paragraph states that Americans who don't control their credit-card spending end up in debt and with huge interest payments. You can infer from this that the "yet potentially dangerous" reference to credit cards means there are drawbacks to credit cards if they are not used in a controlled way.
2. "...imply when..."	The word *imply* suggests that the answer to the question is not stated directly in the text of the article.

3. the idea that credit cards are so convenient and easy to use the statement that people who don't control their spending end up in debt and burdened with huge interest payments	These two ideas lead you to make the correct inference. You see that the ease of using credit cards is what entices people to use them in the first place, and the fact that people tend to overspend as they use credit cards puts them into debt. So you conclude there are drawbacks to credit cards if they are not used in a controlled way.

Answers to 2.5

Correct Answer	Explanation
1. three afternoons a week	You can eliminate *when it's raining* because it doesn't seem reasonable. You may recall from the paragraph that Jake brought the pets three times a week.
2. residents	You can eliminate *children* and *teenagers* because the paragraph is talking about a care center, so "residents" seems like a lot more reasonable answer.
3. They make some people more lively and calm others.	You can eliminate the *mailman* option because it is unrelated to the topic. You'll probably remember that the pets had a positive effect on the residents. If so, you can eliminate the *frighten the residents* option, too.
4. workers in the center	You can eliminate the *local police officer* because it doesn't seem reasonable that an officer would be at a care center. *The attending doctor* could be a reasonable answer, but you may remember that it was the workers in the care center who noticed the changes.

Answers to 2.6

Correct Answer	Explanation
1. main point	The words *main point* tell you that you are being asked to summarize what the paragraph is about.
2. say that control over incoming phone calls has been further improved	A summary of this paragraph should say that control over incoming phone calls has been further improved. This is the most important idea of the paragraph — and you should always include the most important idea in your summary.
3. **Summary 1**	*Phone-number display units give phone owners more control over incoming calls by allowing them to see the name and phone number of the person calling.* This is the better summary, because it captures in one simple statement what the paragraph is about. The other summary misses the main point about giving phone owners control over incoming calls. Instead, it gets sidetracked on a detail that shouldn't be included in a summary.

Chapter **3**

Evaluating Ideas

Learn how to evaluate ideas and decide whether the author provides good arguments to support his or her position.

3.1 Reading with a Purpose

Having a **purpose** for reading helps you focus on the information you want to get from your reading. Whenever you evaluate ideas, your main purpose is to decide if the author provides good arguments to prove that his or her **position** is true.

In most cases, however, you will also have another purpose: the reason you are reading about a specific topic in the first place.

Here are some reasons why people read persuasive articles.

Nelson

I often read persuasive articles because I'm studying a topic for school. A lot of the papers I write require me to form an opinion.

Corinne

I'll read about an issue when I need help making a personal decision. For instance, a persuasive article might help me decide whether I want to recycle my garbage.

---

purpose

A purpose is your reason for reading. You have many purposes for reading. Sometimes you might read an article for pure entertainment. At other times, you might be reading because you need help with a specific task, such as deciding what movie to see or preparing your taxes.

position

The author's position is the stand he or she takes on a topic. In most cases, the author's position will be an opinion about the way things are or how they ought to be.

![checkmark] **Check Your Understanding 3.1**

Put a check (✓) next to the correct answers in the answer column.

Question	Answer
1. If your purpose for reading is to choose a good movie to see this evening, which article would be most helpful?	___ an article that describes the special effects in a recent movie ___ an article that describes and rates all the movies playing at local theaters this week ___ an article that describes the movies that have earned the most profits at the box office over the past 20 years
2. If your purpose for reading is to learn about museums in Culverton City, which publication would be most helpful?	___ an article that describes the new wing in the Walcott Mining Museum ___ *Recommendations for Museum Funding in Culverton City* ___ *A Guide to Museums in Culverton City*
3. If your purpose for reading is to decide which type of car to buy, which resource would be most useful?	___ an article in the automotive section of the paper, describing a car model you are interested in ___ an article in a consumer magazine, comparing different models of cars ___ the sales brochures you receive from car dealers

3.2 Identifying the Author's Position

author's position

The author's position is the stand he or she takes on a topic. In most cases, the author's position will be an opinion about the way things are or how they ought to be. In a piece of persuasive writing, all the ideas work together to prove or support the author's position.

Identifying the **author's position** is an important part of evaluating ideas. You can't decide if an article is convincing until you figure out what the author is trying to say. Identifying the author's position means more than just locating it in a paragraph or article. As a reader, you combine your own knowledge with the ideas from a passage to figure out the author's position.

There are several tactics you can use to identify the author's position:

- making **predictions**
- asking yourself questions
- looking for words that reveal the author's attitude

See how the people below identify the author's position.

predictions

A prediction is a guess you make about what ideas a reading selection might contain before you read the selection. Predicting the author's position can help you stay focused while you read.

Tai

I find it helpful to predict what the author's position *might* be. When I read the article, I check to see if my prediction matches the author's position. Even if it doesn't, thinking about my prediction helps me stay interested and gives me something to look for while I read. This makes it easier to figure out what the author's position really is.

Alonso

I ask myself, "What is the author trying to convince me to believe?" or "What is the author trying to say in this article?"

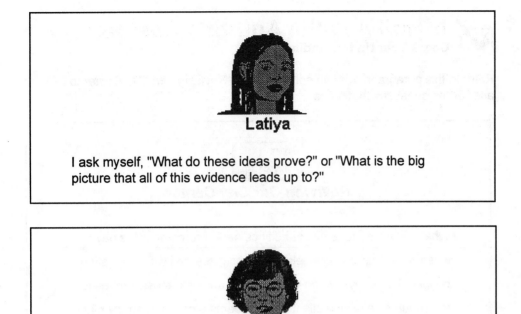

Latiya

I ask myself, "What do these ideas prove?" or "What is the big picture that all of this evidence leads up to?"

Miko

I look for words that show how the author really feels. For instance, if the author says, "We must examine this *short-sighted* policy," I can tell that he or she will probably take a stand against that policy. By using the word *short-sighted,* the author lets me know that he or she thinks the policy will be harmful in the long run.

▶ **Tip:** If you complete all of the tactics above and still can't identify the author's position, try reviewing Chapter 1: Understanding Ideas. It provides basic strategies that can also help.

 **Check Your Understanding 3.2**

Refer to this paragraph from an editorial called *Reviving Our City Center* to answer the questions that follow.

Reviving Our City Center

What can we do to revive our city center? I remember the days when on evenings and weekends the city teemed with interesting people. Nowadays, when work is over, there's a mass exodus to the suburbs, leaving a silent city. It seems a cold and empty place, devoid of intimate feeling. Part of the problem is our insatiable appetite for new things. We demolish old buildings with character to make way for reflective glass monstrosities. Not that I'm against new buildings, but second thought should be given to renovating old structures, thus helping maintain the atmosphere and heritage of our city. Sprucing up City Park is also an option that should be reviewed, along with any suggestions that would make the city a more pleasurable place to spend leisure time. By implementing a few of these ideas, we may once again begin to breathe life into the city and entice people back there.

Put a check (✓) next to the correct answers in the answer column.

Question	Answer
1. Which of these statements describes the author's position?	___ We should improve the atmosphere in the city center without destroying its heritage. ___ We should avoid going into the city during the evenings and on the weekends. ___ We should move back to the city from the suburbs.
2. Which of the following statements would the author be most likely to AGREE with?	___ The city council should approve funds to encourage the building of new office buildings ___ The city council should approve funds to restore older buildings that could be used as theaters, museums, or other cultural centers. ___ The city council should approve funds for a new rapid-transit system that would operate during the work week.
3. Which of these plans would the author be most likely to DISAGREE with?	___ plans for a cycling path by the river ___ a street market on Saturdays ___ demolishing the old library and building a new one

Topics Related to: Identifying the Author's Position

1.5.1 Including Important Ideas

3.3 Identifying Underlying Assumptions

In persuasive writing, authors often make **assumptions**. If these assumptions are not valid, then the ideas an author has expressed may not be valid either. Authors usually don't tell you that they are making assumptions. You have to evaluate their ideas yourself to decide what assumptions are being made and whether they are valid.

assumptions

Assumptions are the unstated ideas upon which an argument, claim, or statement is based.

For instance, the idea that "tough laws stop crime" cannot be valid unless you *assume* that people obey laws or that governments are able to enforce the tough laws.

▶ To identify an author's underlying assumptions, try these tactics:

- Ask yourself questions.
- Look for words that reveal the author's attitude.
- Use your relevant background knowledge and experience.

See how the people below would use these tactics.

Hamid

I'd ask myself, "What does the author want me to believe?" Then I'd ask myself, "What does the author say about this idea?" and "What *doesn't* he or she say about it?"

Yuma

I'd ask myself, "What things that *aren't* written down would have to be valid in order for what *is* written down to be valid?" and "What does the author take for granted?"

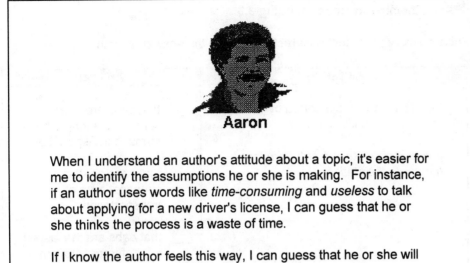

Aaron

When I understand an author's attitude about a topic, it's easier for me to identify the assumptions he or she is making. For instance, if an author uses words like *time-consuming* and *useless* to talk about applying for a new driver's license, I can guess that he or she thinks the process is a waste of time.

If I know the author feels this way, I can guess that he or she will make assumptions that favor the idea of changing or even eliminating the process of applying for a new license.

Rosa

To identify an underlying assumption, I need to think about what *isn't* written down in a text. It helps if I ask myself what I already know about the topic and whether the author's ideas match my own knowledge and experience.

Even if I don't know much about a specific topic, my general knowledge about life or human nature sometimes helps. For instance, I know that it's hard to solve a problem unless the people involved agree to cooperate. If the author's solution requires community involvement, I can look to see if the article *shows* that people will cooperate or if it just *assumes* they will.

Check Your Understanding 3.3

Put a check (✓) next to the correct answers in the answer column.

Question	Answer
1. This statement is supported by which of the following assumptions? *If time is short, take a cab from the theater to the station.*	____ that cabs are more comfortable than other forms of transportation ____ that cabs are the cheapest form of transportation ____ that cabs are the fastest form of transportation
2. Which of the following assumptions provides direct support for this statement? *Making public places smoke-free will improve the health of the nation.*	____ people are more health-conscious today ____ smoking causes illness ____ fewer people smoke today than 20 years ago
3. Which of the following assumptions provides direct support for this statement? *If the profits of Stubbs' department store are to improve, the owners will have to update the product line.*	____ department stores have too many employees and don't make a good profit ____ people are not buying at Stubbs' because the product is old-fashioned ____ people are not buying at Stubbs' because the economy is poor

3.4 Classifying Evidence

Authors use **evidence** to convince readers that their position is valid. By classifying evidence, you get a better sense of the *kind* of information an article contains. This makes it easier to decide if an article is really convincing.

To classify evidence, you sort it into general categories.

- **examples:** specific things or ideas that illustrate an author's position
- **facts:** things that can be seen, observed, or verified
- **quotes:** statements from people who have knowledge or experience
- **opinions:** statements that cannot be verified, but that may make sense to you

Read people's comments to learn more about each type of evidence.

---

evidence

Evidence is the information people use to make decisions. Authors put evidence in their writing as a way of influencing people's decisions. They hope that the information in their book or article will persuade readers to agree with them.

Nelson

Just about anything can be used as an **example** as long as it demonstrates that what the author describes actually does occur or exist. An author who says "some flowers are yellow" might use dandelions, daffodils, and sunflowers as examples. Since these kinds of flowers are often yellow, they support the author's statement.

Yuma

The **facts** authors use often come from studies, surveys, or history. Statements of fact aren't necessarily true; they're just called "facts" because we can go out and verify them. Usually, I'll believe a fact if I trust the place it came from. For example, I am more likely to believe a number from a scientific study than a number from a telephone poll. Other people may feel just the opposite.

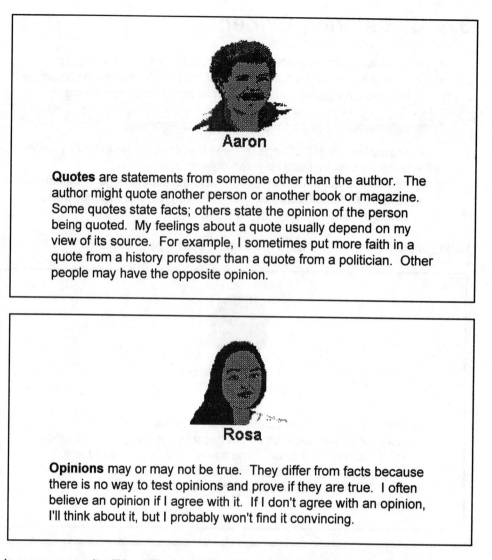

Aaron

Quotes are statements from someone other than the author. The author might quote another person or another book or magazine. Some quotes state facts; others state the opinion of the person being quoted. My feelings about a quote usually depend on my view of its source. For example, I sometimes put more faith in a quote from a history professor than a quote from a politician. Other people may have the opposite opinion.

Rosa

Opinions may or may not be true. They differ from facts because there is no way to test opinions and prove if they are true. I often believe an opinion if I agree with it. If I don't agree with an opinion, I'll think about it, but I probably won't find it convincing.

In some cases, it will be difficult to tell which category a piece of evidence belongs in. For instance, an author may list some examples that are also facts — and it will be hard to decide which category to pick. Don't worry about this too much. It's the process of thinking about evidence and deciding what category it *probably* belongs in that matters most. It helps you work with the article's ideas so you can evaluate them closely.

▶ **Tip:** You don't always have to agree with an author just because he or she gives facts and figures. Often, writers will only choose evidence that supports their position. If the ideas in an article don't make sense to you, it's a good idea to investigate further, — even if the author does use facts, examples, and quotes.

✔ **Check Your Understanding 3.4**

Put a check (✓) next to the correct answers in the answer column. More than one answer may be correct for each question.

Question	Answer
1. Classify the evidence in this sentence as example, fact, quote, or opinion. *Bicycling is an enjoyable form of exercise.*	____ example ____ fact ____ quote ____ opinion
2. Classify the evidence in this sentence as example, fact, quote, or opinion. *The direct forerunner of the modern bicycle was the French velocipede, a crank-driven machine, which became popular in France about 1855.*	____ example ____ fact ____ quote ____ opinion
3. Classify the evidence in this sentence as example, fact, quote, or opinion. *According to Greg LeMond, three-time winner of the Tour-de-France, "If you are riding primarily for health reasons, I recommend graduating to touring."*	____ example ____ fact ____ quote ____ opinion
4. Classify the evidence in this sentence as example, fact, quote, or opinion. *In the mid-1980s, approximately 82 million bicycles were being ridden in the United States.*	____ example ____ fact ____ quote ____ opinion
5. Classify the evidence in these sentences as example, fact, quote, or opinion. *Different types of bicycles have become popular over the years for different types of recreational activities. During the 1980s, the most popular bicycle was the ten-speed touring bike. Mountain bikes with fat tires became increasingly popular as all-terrain bikes.*	____ example ____ fact ____ quote ____ opinion

3.5 Reading Outlines

Reading an **outline** of ideas from an article can help you evaluate the article and decide whether it's convincing. When you see the author's arguments in a brief outline, you can picture the way the ideas in the article work together to support the author's position. Because all of the ideas are organized, it's easier to tell when some of them don't have enough support.

An outline contains

- the author's position
- arguments and reasons
- evidence

Read what each person below has to say about the contents of a brief outline of arguments.

outline

Outlines are one way of organizing the most important ideas from an article. An outline contains brief statements of the author's main message and the ideas that support it.

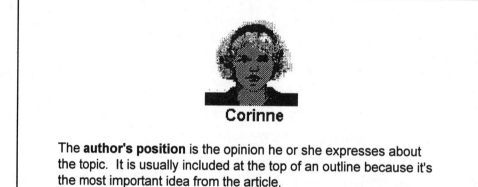

Corinne

The **author's position** is the opinion he or she expresses about the topic. It is usually included at the top of an outline because it's the most important idea from the article.

Alonso

Arguments and reasons are the ideas authors use to convince you to agree with them. These ideas support the author's position by explaining it or giving evidence to demonstrate that it's valid. When you read the arguments and reasons in an outline, you can tell if the author has really supported his or her position.

Latiya

Evidence is the information people use to make decisions. Authors put evidence in their writing as a way of influencing people's decisions. When I read the author's evidence in an outline, I can tell if the ideas are backed up by facts, examples, quotes, or opinions.

To learn more about the outline below, refer to the number labels on the outline and read the descriptions that follow.

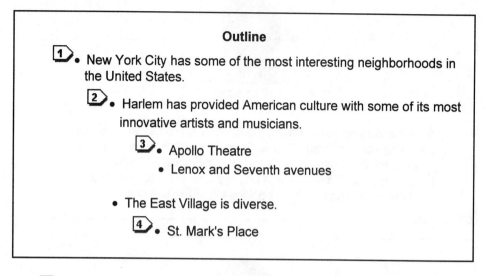

Outline

1. • New York City has some of the most interesting neighborhoods in the United States.

   2. • Harlem has provided American culture with some of its most innovative artists and musicians.

      3. • Apollo Theatre
         • Lenox and Seventh avenues

   • The East Village is diverse.

      4. • St. Mark's Place

---

1 **New York City has some of the most interesting neighborhoods in the United States.**

This is the author's position. It appears at the top of an outline because it is the most important idea from the article or paragraph.

2 **Harlem has provided American culture with some of its most innovative artists and musicians.**

This is one of the author's arguments or reasons. By showing how artists from one neighborhood (Harlem) have influenced American culture, the author hopes to convince you that New York's neighborhoods are interesting.

In an outline of arguments, the arguments and reasons appear below the author's position. They are usually indented.

3 **Apollo Theatre**

The Apollo Theatre is an example of how Harlem's artists have influenced many aspects of American culture. Some of the most talented musical artists in the U.S. have performed there, including Billie Holiday, Duke Ellington, and Aretha Franklin.

In an outline of arguments, examples and other kinds of evidence appear below the idea they support. Sometimes evidence appears directly below the author's position. In other cases, it supports one of the author's arguments or reasons. Evidence is usually indented a bit more than the idea it helps to prove.

4 **St. Mark's Place**

This is evidence the author uses to show that the East Village is diverse. In an actual article or paragraph, an author wouldn't just say "St. Mark's

Place." There would be one or two sentences describing why St. Mark's Place proves that the East Village is diverse.

When people write outlines, they substitute short sentences and phrases for the ideas they read in the article.

Here is the article that goes with this outline.

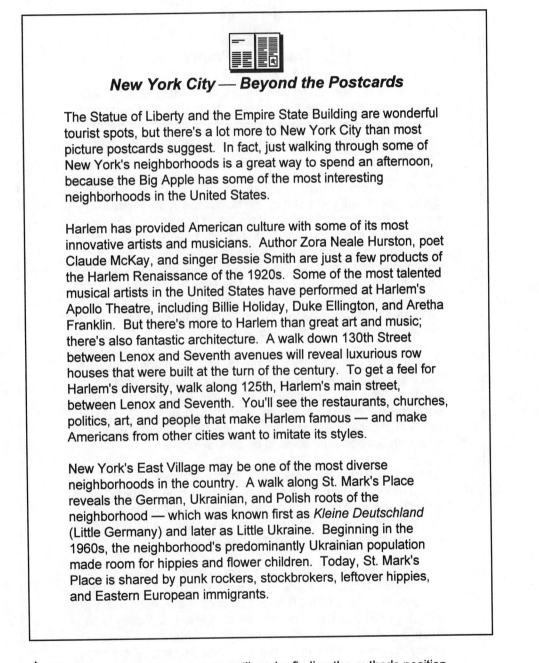

New York City — Beyond the Postcards

The Statue of Liberty and the Empire State Building are wonderful tourist spots, but there's a lot more to New York City than most picture postcards suggest. In fact, just walking through some of New York's neighborhoods is a great way to spend an afternoon, because the Big Apple has some of the most interesting neighborhoods in the United States.

Harlem has provided American culture with some of its most innovative artists and musicians. Author Zora Neale Hurston, poet Claude McKay, and singer Bessie Smith are just a few products of the Harlem Renaissance of the 1920s. Some of the most talented musical artists in the United States have performed at Harlem's Apollo Theatre, including Billie Holiday, Duke Ellington, and Aretha Franklin. But there's more to Harlem than great art and music; there's also fantastic architecture. A walk down 130th Street between Lenox and Seventh avenues will reveal luxurious row houses that were built at the turn of the century. To get a feel for Harlem's diversity, walk along 125th, Harlem's main street, between Lenox and Seventh. You'll see the restaurants, churches, politics, art, and people that make Harlem famous — and make Americans from other cities want to imitate its styles.

New York's East Village may be one of the most diverse neighborhoods in the country. A walk along St. Mark's Place reveals the German, Ukrainian, and Polish roots of the neighborhood — which was known first as *Kleine Deutschland* (Little Germany) and later as Little Ukraine. Beginning in the 1960s, the neighborhood's predominantly Ukrainian population made room for hippies and flower children. Today, St. Mark's Place is shared by punk rockers, stockbrokers, leftover hippies, and Eastern European immigrants.

▶ **Tip:** You can create your own outlines by finding the author's position, arguments, and evidence and then writing them up in an outline form. Creating an outline helps you think about the ideas in an article and how they are organized.

Check Your Understanding 3.5

Refer to the article and outline below to answer the questions that follow. Put a check (✓) next to the correct answers in the answer column.

Trash it or Profit?

It's time we did something with the landfill on the west side of town, as it's been full for more than a year. Covering it with earth and turning it into a green area is one possibility worth considering. Many cities in other areas of the country have done this quite successfully.

As you drive down Wilson Way an unsightly view meets the eye — the landfill. It really is a blot on the landscape in an otherwise pleasant part of town. Local people report that children frequently play near the site, and some have actually been seen on the dump itself. This should be a real concern to parents and to the community as a whole, as the health risks are obvious. Another spin-off that is apparent to anyone who lives near the landfill, or to anyone who has been in the vicinity, is the horrible smell that emanates from this eyesore. It can be quite nauseating and makes me wonder how the locals manage to live there.

Taking a look at the facilities of the city of Dennington, it is obvious that the town is short on outdoor recreational areas. Since Skidmore Park and Evergreen Golf Course were sold to housing developers, the city's current parks and golf courses have been overly subscribed. Consequently, a new recreational area such as a park and/or golf course would be most welcome.

Adding a park or golf course would greatly improve the neighborhood. The beautiful and calm environment created by a golf course would make the neighborhood a nicer place to live. Property values in the area would also increase, and it could once again become a desirable place to buy a home.

There have been critics who claim such a project would be too expensive. Of course, there would be the initial cost of covering and greening the landfill. Then the cosmetics of turning it into a park or golf course would have to be completed. If money is an issue, a golf course should be a serious consideration. Over a period of years, other cities have recouped the costs of greening a landfill with golf club membership and green fees.

Outline

- We should turn the full landfill into a green area.
  - The landfill is unsightly and unhealthy.
    - blot on the landscape
    - children play near it
    - horrible smell
  - The city needs a new recreation area.
    - city is short of parks and golf courses
  - Improve the neighborhood
    - nicer place to live
    - property values increase
  - Low cost project
    - fee-paying golf course

Question	Answer
1. What is the author's main point?	____ We should keep children off the landfill. ____ We should turn the full landfill into a green area. ____ We should start another landfill.
2. Which are arguments or reasons that support the author's position?	____ Filling the landfill will improve the neighborhood. ____ Filling the landfill will be expensive. ____ Filling the landfill will take a long time.
3. Which of the following provide evidence for the author's claim that turning the landfill into a green area would improve the neighborhood?	____ Local people report that children play near the site. ____ The city's parks are already too busy. ____ Filling the landfill will increase property values.

Topics Related to: Reading Outlines

4.3 Using Idea Maps

3.6 Summing Up Ideas

summarize

Summarizing means restating what you've read in a shortened form, keeping only the most important ideas. You can summarize any piece of writing: a sentence, a paragraph, a section of text, an article, or an entire book.

Evaluating an article often requires you to **summarize** ideas. Summarizing means restating in a shortened form what you've read , keeping only the most important ideas.

Sometimes you need to find the **most important idea** in a paragraph or section of text. At other times, you need to sum up your own opinions about the article itself.

When you are asked to summarize or find a summary statement, try looking for a sentence or paragraph that briefly states what the text is all about. When a piece of writing *doesn't* contain its own summary, you need to read all of the ideas and then state the most important message in your own words.

most important idea

The most important idea is the main message that a piece of writing expresses — the one idea that ties together all of the ideas you have read. The most important idea is sometimes called the main point or main idea.

▶ To summarize a section of text:

- Find the **most important idea** from your reading.
- Include information that is needed to explain this idea.
- Eliminate unnecessary details.

When you are asked to evaluate the ideas in a paragraph or article, it helps to take time to summarize the opinions and decisions you made while evaluating the text.

▶ To summarize your ideas, look over the text, a **map or outline** of ideas from the text, and/or your notes. Then ask yourself the following questions:

map or outline

Maps and outlines are two kinds of organizers that give you a picture of the important ideas from an article. When you read a map or outline, you see the ideas that will help you sum up your opinion of the article. For more information, see section 3.5 of this chapter.

- Is the **author's position** even worth arguing?
- Do the reasons or arguments make the position convincing?
- Are the author's ideas supported by **examples, facts, quotes, or opinions**?

If you answer "yes" to most of these questions, you probably found the passage convincing. If you answer "no," then you probably weren't convinced. If your answers are mixed, then you probably found the passage somewhat convincing.

▶ **Tip**: More detailed information about summarizing is provided in Chapter 1, section 5 of this Handbook.

Look at what each person has to say to learn more good questions to ask yourself.

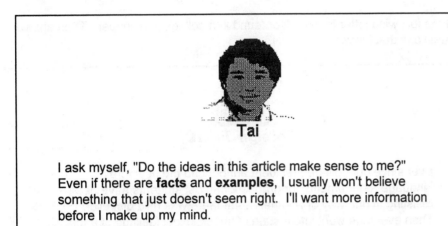

Tai

I ask myself, "Do the ideas in this article make sense to me?" Even if there are **facts** and **examples**, I usually won't believe something that just doesn't seem right. I'll want more information before I make up my mind.

facts

Facts are a type of evidence authors use to persuade people to agree with them. They are things that can be seen, observed, or verified.

examples

Examples are a type of evidence authors use to influence people's decisions. They are specific things or ideas that illustrate an author's position.

Miko

I ask myself this question, "Does the text contain statements that weaken the **author's position**?" If the answer is "yes," I make sure the author explains those statements and successfully argues against them. If he or she doesn't do this, I won't find the article very convincing.

author's position

The author's position is the stand he or she takes on a topic. In most cases, the author's position will be an opinion about the way things are or how they ought to be. In a piece of persuasive writing, all the ideas work together to prove or support the author's position.

Rosa

I ask myself whether the author has successfully answered *my* questions.

As I read, I often come up with my own questions, such as "Will the author clarify this point?" or "This is an assumption — will the author prove that it's true?" My questions are important. If an author doesn't answer them, I won't always find the article convincing.

Check Your Understanding 3.6

summarize

Summarizing means restating what you've read in a shortened form, keeping only the most important ideas. You can summarize any piece of writing: a sentence, a paragraph, a section of text, an article, or an entire book.

Read the following letter to the editor found in a college newspaper. Then answer the questions that follow.

Foreign Jitters

1   Ever since our college president announced the new foreign-language requirements for graduation, most students have been resisting in one way or another. First there was mild disbelief. Then everyone went into a state of shock. Now feelings of anger and panic have settled in around campus. "I don't have time for foreign-language classes." "Why do I need to take a foreign language? It doesn't have anything to do with my major." "I'm already having trouble passing my English classes. How will I ever master a foreign language?" And so goes the long list of complaints and concerns.

2   But have we got our heads in the sand, or what? Has anybody been reading the papers lately? In case you haven't noticed, we are part of an increasingly competitive global economy. We can either climb on board and become part of that economy, or it's going to pass us by. An important part of being competitive in the global economy is communicating effectively with our potential customers — customers who may speak Spanish or Japanese or Russian or Chinese. Just last week, I was talking to an exchange student from Japan. When she graduates, she plans to return to her country and work for Sanyo, creating marketing plans for their new products. Don't you think she has an edge over her American counterparts who don't speak a word of Japanese and have no understanding of other cultures?

3   And those of you native-speakers who are having trouble with your English classes, will never really understand English until you view it from the perspective of another language. It's easy to ignore the structure inherent in English. After all, you've been speaking it your whole life. But when you learn another language, you're forced to tackle language head-on, because it's all new. You quickly turn to English as a welcome and familiar comparison for the new structure you are learning.

---

4   I recently heard someone say he didn't know what an infinitive was, or the difference between the subjective and objective case in English, until he studied a foreign language. And if you don't know what they are either, I rest my case. You could, if you studied a foreign language.

5   An important advantage of studying a foreign language, one that shouldn't be overlooked, is gaining an understanding and awareness of the cultures behind the languages. Edward T. Hall, an anthropologist and author of *The Silent Language*, claims that culture is a silent language every bit as significant as spoken language. If we are to interact successfully with those who speak other languages, and avoid unfortunate misunderstandings, we need to study the culture as well. Studying foreign languages gives us a good opportunity to become familiar with other cultures.

6   I must admit that I too panicked, when I first heard the president's announcement about the new language requirements. But I've since decided there are some compelling and urgent reasons for this change, such as helping us become competitive in a global economy, helping us understand our own language better, and helping us be more sensitive to other cultures. And I, for one, intend to support this new requirement and give it the "good ol' college try."

Put a check (✓) next to the correct answers in the answer column.

Question	Answer
1. Which paragraph best summarizes the author's position?	___ Paragraph 1 ___ Paragraph 2 ___ Paragraph 6
2. What is the author's position or **most important idea**?	___ Students need to take more English classes to fulfill the graduation requirements. ___ Students should support the new foreign-language requirement. ___ Students should read the papers more often.

author's position

The author's position is the stand he or she takes on a topic. In most cases, the author's position will be an opinion about the way things are or how they ought to be. In a piece of persuasive writing, all the ideas work together to prove or support the author's position.

most important idea

The most important idea is the main message that a piece of writing expresses — the one idea that ties together all of the ideas you have read. The most important idea is sometimes called the main point or main idea.

3. What reason did the author give first to support his position?	___ Students need to learn a foreign language to understand their own. ___ Students need to learn a foreign language to learn about other cultures. ___ Students need to learn a foreign language to compete in a global economy.
4. In paragraph 2, the author makes the point that in order to compete in a global economy, we need to be able to communicate effectively with our global customers. Which evidence does he use to support his point?	___ The author tells how people aren't reading the papers. ___ The author describes how a Japanese exchange student is preparing for the global economy. ___ The author compares Americans to the Spanish, Russians, and Chinese.
5. The author could probably strengthen his position in paragraph 2 by doing which of the following?	___ telling a story about how difficult it is to learn English ___ giving an example to illustrate how the Spanish view time differently than most Americans ___ citing some statistics about global competition

6. What evidence does the author use in paragraph 4 to support the idea that learning another language will help you understand English better?	___ The author describes the difference between the subjective and objective case in English. ___ The author describes how difficult it is for someone to learn a foreign language. ___ The author describes someone who finally understood several difficult concepts about English by studying another language.
7. What evidence does the author use to support the idea that learning about other cultures is an important part of learning to speak another language?	___ The author quotes an expert saying that culture is an important form of language. ___ The author points out that we should all be able to interact successfully with those who speak other languages. ___ The author admits that he too panicked when he first heard about the language requirements.
8. A student who read the letter to the editor summed up her feelings about the article by saying that she still didn't think learning a language was important for her. She was more concerned about finding a job and paying off her car than competing in the global economy. Which of these reasons would strengthen the author's position the most for students with similar concerns?	___ Learning a foreign language, along with your other skills, can provide you with more job opportunities. ___ Learning a foreign language can make you a more knowledgeable traveler. ___ Learning a foreign language can be a fun and gratifying experience.

Topics Related to:	Summing Up Ideas
	4.3 Using Idea Maps

3.7 Answers to Questions

Answers to 3.1

Correct Answer	Explanation
1. an article that describes and rates all the movies playing in local theaters this week	An article that describes and rates all the movies playing in local theaters this week will help you decide which movies you may want to see. This article will allow you to see <u>all</u> the choices before you make your decision. An article that only describes the special effects in one movie doesn't tell you which movies are currently playing. An article describing the movies that have earned the most profits over the past 20 years does not necessarily give you any information about what's playing in town.
2. *A Guide to Museums in Culverton City*	A *Guide to Museums in Culverton City* gives you information about all the museums in the city. You don't want to read about only one museum (the article describing the Walcott Mining Museum), and you don't need to know about funding for museums.
3. an article in a consumer magazine, comparing different models of cars	The article in the consumer magazine will give you access to information about many different cars. This will help you compare the advantages and disadvantages of different models. The article in the paper provides only limited information about one model of car. Although the sales brochures could be a source of comparative information, you would have to gather brochures for many different models. Even then, it may still be difficult, if not impossible, to know how to compare this information. You also have to remember that information you get from a car dealer will be biased and might not focus on features of the car in which you are interested.

Answers to 3.2

Correct Answer	Explanation
1. We should improve the atmosphere in the city center without destroying its heritage.	The author gives several examples of how the city center could be improved without destroying its heritage.
2. The city council should approve funds to help restore older buildings that could be used as theaters, museums, or other cultural centers.	The author's emphasis seems to be to renovate what is already there in order to preserve the city's heritage. Therefore, the author would most likely support the city council's plan to help restore old buildings, and use them as places where people could spend leisure time. The author would probably not approve of plans to provide funds encouraging the building of more new office buildings in the city center or for providing a new rapid-transit system to be operated only during the work week.
3. demolishing the old library and building a new one	The author would likely approve of plans to create a cycling path by the river or a street market on Saturdays. These are both ways of improving the atmosphere in the city. The author feels that old buildings should be renovated, where possible, and would probably disagree with demolishing the old library and building a new one.

Answers to 3.3

Correct Answer	Explanation
1. that cabs are the fastest form of transportation	The author assumes that cabs are the fastest form of transportation. The suggestion is made to use a cab when time is short.
2. smoking causes illness	This statement must be true if the sentence is true. Making public places smoke-free cannot improve the health of the nation unless smoking causes illness.

3. people are not buying at Stubbs' because the product is old-fashioned	The author assumes that people are not buying at Stubbs' because the product is old-fashioned. If the profits of Stubbs' department store are to improve, the owners will have to update the product line.

Answers to 3.4

Correct Answer	Explanation
1. opinion	This is an opinion. Not everyone would find bicycling enjoyable.
2. fact	This is a fact because the information can be verified. By looking in history books, you can check to see if the velocipede was the direct forerunner of the modern bicycle, and if it was popular in France about 1855.
3. quote opinion	The quotation marks and the words "according to" tell you that this is a quote from Greg LeMond, three-time winner of the Tour-de-France bike race. This is Greg LeMond's opinion, because it is hard to determine if touring has better health effects than other forms of biking.
4. fact	This is a fact because it gives numbers that can be verified. To see if it is true, you can check books and magazines on cycling.
5. fact example	This is a fact because it can be verified. To see if it is true, you can check sales records, cycling books, and magazines. Examples of two types of bikes are given to show how different types of bicycles have been used over the years for different recreational activities.

Answers to 3.5

Correct Answer	Explanation
1. We should turn the full landfill into a green area.	This is the author's main point or position. It is the most important idea in an outline, so it always appears at the top. In most cases, the author's position won't be indented as much as the other, less important ideas.
2. Filling the landfill will improve the neighborhood.	This is an argument that supports the author's position. In an outline, arguments appear below the author's position.
3. Filling the landfill will increase property values.	"Increase property values" is evidence showing that the neighborhood can be improved.

Answers to 3.6

Correct Answer	Explanation
1. Paragraph 6	The author doesn't state his position or most important idea until the last sentence in paragraph 6: "And I, for one, intend to support this new requirement and give it 'the good ol' college try'." This paragraph also summarizes his reasons or arguments for this position. He argues that studying foreign languages will help us: • become competitive in a global economy • understand our own language better • be more sensitive to other cultures
2. Students should support the new foreign-language requirement.	The author is trying to convince students to support the new foreign-language requirement. The introductory paragraph suggests that dissent is a big problem and outlines some of the reasons for this dissent. In the rest of the letter, the author tries to provide reasons that answer some of these criticisms in order to gain support for the new requirement.

3. Students need to learn a foreign language to compete in a global economy.	This is the first reason the author gives to support his position. This reason is presented in paragraph 2.
4. He describes how a Japanese exchange student is preparing for the global economy.	The author uses an example about an exchange student from Japan. He shows how her preparation, learning a language and a culture, will help her be more competitive in the global economy.
5. citing some statistics about global competition	The author might make his opinions more credible by adding some specific facts — statistics that can be verified by referring to credible sources. For example: "In case you haven't noticed, we are part of an increasingly competitive global economy," could be backed up by some recent statistics about the U.S. trade deficit.
6. He describes someone who finally understood several difficult concepts about English by studying another language.	The author quotes what he heard one student say about how studying a foreign language helped him understand English. In this case, quoting another student would probably be considered successful evidence, because students may find his insights useful and believable. In other cases, it may be more effective to use an expert's quote to give the evidence more credibility.
7. He quotes an expert saying that culture is an important form of language.	In paragraph 5, the author refers to an opinion by Edward T. Hall, an anthropologist and author of a book called *The Silent Language,* to support the idea that learning about other cultures is an important part of learning to speak another language.
8. Learning a foreign language, along with your other skills, can provide you with more job opportunities.	The reasons given by the author (competing in a global economy and understanding other cultures) may still seem a bit removed from most students' immediate, personal concerns. Showing how learning a foreign language can increase job opportunities in their chosen fields might be a more compelling argument for most students.

Researching Ideas

Learn how to gather and use information from different articles.

4.1 Researching with a Purpose

Having a **purpose** helps you plan your research. A purpose answers the question, "Why am I doing this research?" and lets you know what kinds of information you should find.

purpose

A purpose is your reason for doing research. You have many purposes for researching topics. As a student, you may do research before writing a paper. In other parts of your life, research can help you make decisions about what you should eat, who you should vote for, or how you should spend your money.

A purpose helps you:

- decide what the topic of your research should be
- choose research sources
- come up with some questions that your research should answer
- stay focused while you read

Read how purposes help the following people plan their research.

Corinne

Once I know *why* I'm doing research, it's easier to decide what the topic of my research should be. For instance, if my purpose is to figure out why I feel so tired in the morning and afternoons, then the topic of my research might be "sleep," "causes of sleepiness," or "how to tell if you're getting enough sleep."

Tai

My purpose for researching helps me pick out the books and articles I should read. If my purpose is to get the best deal on a new stereo, for instance, then I wouldn't read just any book or article about stereos. I'd choose sources that specifically discuss the price or the quality of different stereos.

Latiya

Once I understand my purpose for research, I ask myself, "What questions should my research answer?" or "What do I need to know?"

For example, if my purpose is to learn how to change the oil in my car, my research will need to answer the following questions:

What parts of the automobile do I need to know about?
Where do I purchase supplies?
Do I need special tools?
What are the steps for putting in new oil?

Alonso

While I am reading books and articles, I keep my purpose for research in mind. As I read, I look for ideas that will meet the needs of my purpose or answer my research questions.

For example, my purpose might be to find out whether the office where I work should become computerized. As I read, I would look for ideas that show the advantages and disadvantages of using computers in the workplace. I'd also look for answers to questions such as, "How could computers save time?"

Keeping my purpose in mind helps me stay focused on my reading — so I get a lot more out of it.

 **Check Your Understanding 4.1**

Read the purpose below and then answer the following questions.

Purpose:

> *You want to buy a microwave oven. Because your finances are limited, you decide to find out how much microwave ovens cost. You also want to know what options come with each type of oven and how much cooking time you will save by buying a microwave oven.*

Put a check (✓) next to the correct answers in the answer column.

Question	Answer
1. Which would be the best topic of your research?	____ recipes for microwave ovens ____ the cost and functions of different microwave ovens ____ the cheapest microwave oven available
2. Which **two** articles would make the best sources for your research?	____ an article describing the food texture and flavor benefits of cooking with a microwave oven ____ an article comparing the costs and options of microwave ovens ____ an article explaining how microwave ovens work ____ an article examining the cooking times of microwave ovens compared with a regular oven

3. What **two** questions should your research answer?	____ How much do microwave ovens cost, and what options are available?
	____ How do microwave ovens work, and are they able to retain food texture and flavor?
	____ How much time is saved by using a microwave oven instead of a regular oven?

Topics Related to: Researching with a Purpose

3.1 Reading with a Purpose

4.2 Taking Notes

Taking notes helps you find and remember important ideas from your reading. It also gives you a way to quickly look up these ideas later if you don't save the article you read or if you don't have time to read the entire article again.

taking notes

When you take notes, you write down in a separate place the ideas you are reading that are relevant to your research project. You may also write down your own thoughts about the ideas or about additional ideas you want to research.

▶ When you take notes, these ideas are helpful:

- Write down important ideas that summarize what the article is saying.
- Write down ideas that you want to remember or to use in meeting your purpose.
- Use your own words rather than copying exact wording from the article.

See why the people below take notes when they research.

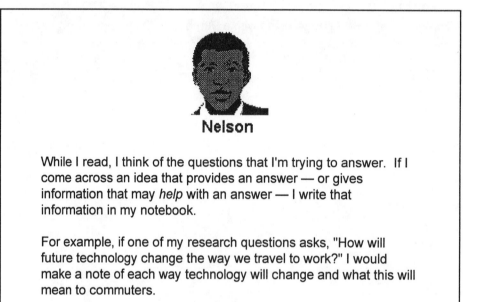

Nelson

While I read, I think of the questions that I'm trying to answer. If I come across an idea that provides an answer — or gives information that may *help* with an answer — I write that information in my notebook.

For example, if one of my research questions asks, "How will future technology change the way we travel to work?" I would make a note of each way technology will change and what this will mean to commuters.

Corinne

I like to add additional comments when I make notes. For example, if I was researching the characteristics of the planet Jupiter and made a note that it was the largest planet in the solar system, I might also make another note saying "Compare its size to the Earth's." That way I would remember that I wanted to find out how large Jupiter is compared to Earth.

Aaron

While I read an article, I stop when I find an idea that I think is important. I try to reword that idea as I write it in my notebook. By putting the idea in my own words, I make sure that I understand the idea, that I'm not just copying words without grasping their meaning.

▶ **Tip:** Sometimes you can also mark text in the article you are reading. Highlighting in the text will also help you find important ideas and remember what you read. But when you can't make marks in an article, you can still write down ideas in a separate place.

 **Check Your Understanding 4.2**

Read the purpose, research questions, and the paragraph below to answer the first question that follows.

Purpose:

You are part of a group that is going to start publishing a community newspaper. You have been asked to give a talk to the group on recent trends and developments and what the future looks like for the newspaper world.

Research questions:
What are the trends and developments in the newspaper world?
What changes are likely in the future?

> *Despite the development of film, radio, and television, newspapers remain a major source of information. It is estimated that eight out of 10 adult Americans read a newspaper every day. The newspaper is an important tool that provides us with information and helps us form opinions. Newspapers have to rely on the publication of advertising for their income. With the loss of advertising revenue in the 20th century, many dailies have gone out of business. The newspaper industry has had to be creative to think of new ways to entice people to buy newspapers. The introduction of the tabloid newspaper in the 20th century has been an attempt to capture more of the market. The tabloids are smaller in size, give a condensed version of the news, and contain more illustrations.*

Put a check (✓) next to the correct answer in the answer column.

Question	Answer
After reading the paragraph, which of these ideas would you place in a notebook?	____ The newspaper is an important tool that provides us with information and helps us form opinions.
	____ The introduction of the tabloid newspaper in the 20th century has been an attempt to catch more of the market.
	____ Newspapers have to rely on the publication of advertising for their income.

 **Check Your Understanding 4.2b**

Put a check (✓) next to the correct answer in the answer column.

Which of these notes would be most helpful if you were researching the feeding habits of butterflies?	___ Winter hibernation is common in snowy climates.
	___ Butterflies seek nectar from flowering plants.
	___ Butterfly wings are often brightly colored.

4.3 Using Idea Maps

Using **idea maps** will help you keep track of the information you have researched. When you see your research organized in a map, you'll be able to picture the way ideas can be put together to fulfill your research purpose. You can also see if you have holes in your research — places where you need more information.

Idea maps contain the most important ideas from your research. As a result, reading idea maps makes it easier to summarize your research.

Look at the comments of each person below to learn more about the contents of a map.

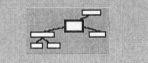

Miko

When I do research, I always come up with a main message — the most important idea I want to express. Idea maps include this message in the center, so that the most important idea is the first idea you notice.

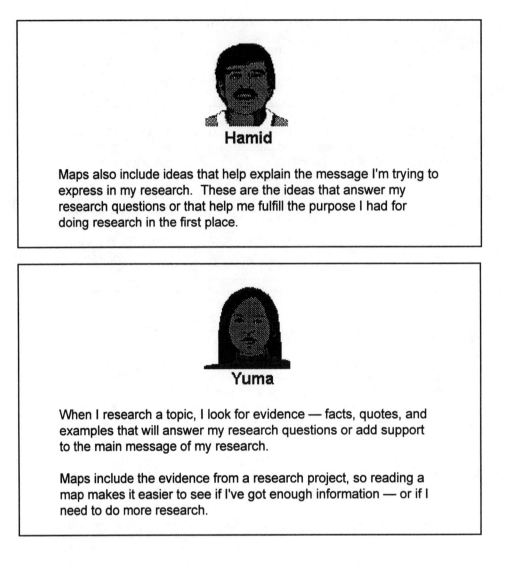

Hamid

Maps also include ideas that help explain the message I'm trying to express in my research. These are the ideas that answer my research questions or that help me fulfill the purpose I had for doing research in the first place.

Yuma

When I research a topic, I look for evidence — facts, quotes, and examples that will answer my research questions or add support to the main message of my research.

Maps include the evidence from a research project, so reading a map makes it easier to see if I've got enough information — or if I need to do more research.

To learn more about how to read the map below, refer to the number labels on the map and read the following descriptions.

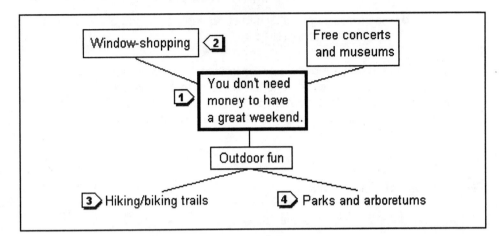

1 You don't need money to have a great weekend.

This is the most important idea for a research project or paper. It appears at the center of the map because it is the most important idea that the research expresses.

The center box of a map is often drawn with darker lines — or the writing in it is larger or bold — in order to give it more emphasis.

2 Window-shopping

This is one of the ideas that support the main message of this research project. It shows that window-shopping is one form of weekend entertainment that doesn't cost money.

In a map, ideas that support each other are connected by lines.

3 Hiking/biking trails

Hiking/biking trails give an example of an outdoor activity that is fun and free. Because this is an example of an outdoor activity, a line connects it to the box that says "outdoor fun."

Some maps also use color to show connections. In a map like this, for example, all of the evidence that supports "outdoor fun" could also be printed in a shade of blue.

4 Parks and arboretums

Parks and arboretums are examples of places you can go for free outdoor fun on the weekends. In an actual research paper or project, you wouldn't just say "parks and arboretums." You would write one or two sentences showing how parks and arboretums can provide a great cost-free weekend.

People who create maps substitute short sentences and phrases for the ideas that have been researched.

▶ **Tip:** You can create your own maps by putting the most important idea from your research into a center box and then adding more boxes that contain the ideas that support it. Creating a map can help you write a summary or a research paper. It can also help you prepare to speak about the research you have done.

 Check Your Understanding 4.3

Refer to the map below to answer the following questions.

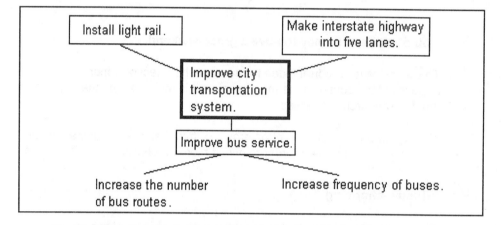

Put a check (✓) next to the correct answers in the answer column.

Question	Answer
1. What is an idea that supports the main message of this research project?	___ Increase the number of bus routes. ___ Improve city transportation system. ___ Improve bus service.
2. What is an example of how the bus service could be improved?	___ Install light rail. ___ Make interstate highway into five lanes. ___ Increase frequency of buses.

Topics Related to: Using Idea Maps

3.5 Reading Outlines

4.4 Summarizing Your Research

Summarizing your research is one way to organize your thoughts and decide which information is most important. When you research a topic, you may also find it helpful to summarize the ideas from the sources you are using. Whenever you summarize, you give a brief statement of the most important ideas — from an article, from part of an article, or from your research project as a whole.

▶ To summarize your research, try these steps:

- State the **most important idea** from your research.
- Include the ideas that are needed to explain it.
- Figure out how different ideas are related.

If you have an **outline** or **idea map** of your research, these steps will have been completed already. All you'll need to do is refer to the outline or map to get the important ideas and then write a sentence or two about them.

Look at the people below to see how and why they summarize their research.

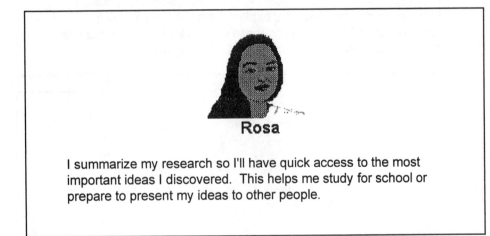

Rosa

I summarize my research so I'll have quick access to the most important ideas I discovered. This helps me study for school or prepare to present my ideas to other people.

summarizing

Summarizing means restating the most important ideas from your research in a brief and clear way. Usually a research summary will be one or two paragraphs long, depending on how much research you have done.

most important idea

When you research a topic, you will probably uncover many important ideas. Usually, however, you'll want to put all of these ideas together and decide on one general idea — one most important statement that all the other ideas support. If you plan to share the results of your research with other people, the most important idea will be the main message that you want to express to them.

outline

Outlines are one way of organizing the most important ideas from an article. An outline contains brief statements of the author's main message and the ideas that support it.

idea map

An idea map is one way of organizing the most important ideas from an article or research project. Idea maps use boxes, lines, and sometimes colors to show how ideas are connected.

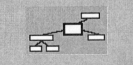

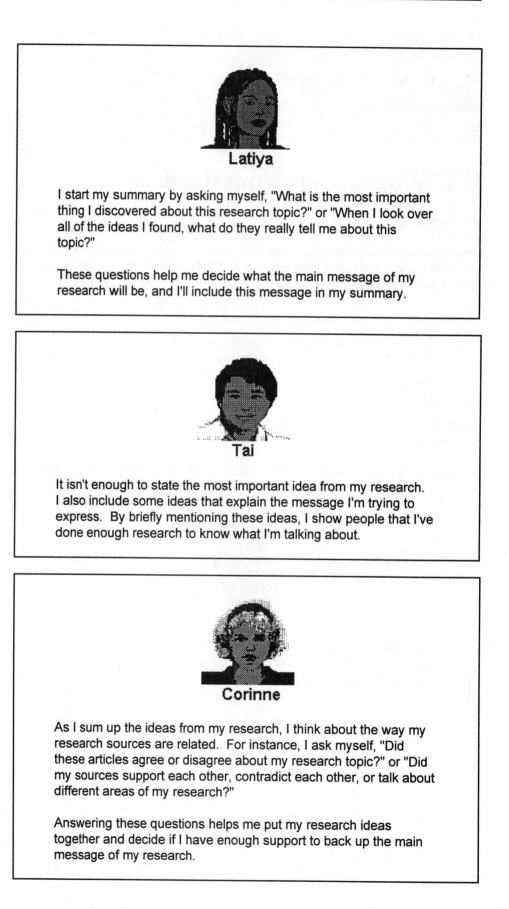

Latiya

I start my summary by asking myself, "What is the most important thing I discovered about this research topic?" or "When I look over all of the ideas I found, what do they really tell me about this topic?"

These questions help me decide what the main message of my research will be, and I'll include this message in my summary.

Tai

It isn't enough to state the most important idea from my research. I also include some ideas that explain the message I'm trying to express. By briefly mentioning these ideas, I show people that I've done enough research to know what I'm talking about.

Corinne

As I sum up the ideas from my research, I think about the way my research sources are related. For instance, I ask myself, "Did these articles agree or disagree about my research topic?" or "Did my sources support each other, contradict each other, or talk about different areas of my research?"

Answering these questions helps me put my research ideas together and decide if I have enough support to back up the main message of my research.

▶ **Tip:** If you would like more detailed information about summarizing, look at Chapter 1, section 5 of this Handbook.

 Check Your Understanding 4.4

Refer to the research below to answer the questions that follow.

Purpose:
Your music club is producing a music fair to help the public understand more about different instruments. You have been asked to find out about the history of the mouth organ, and in what kind of music it is used.

Research questions:
When was the mouth organ invented?
In what kind of music is it used?

Some of the marked ideas:

- The mouth organ that we know today was invented independently in England and Germany during the 1820s. It is a small, oblong box that has a row of air channels. At the end of each channel is a small metal free reed. Musical tones are produced by blowing or suction.

- The free-reed principle was introduced into Europe in 1777, in the form of the Chinese mouth organ.

- The instrument is used in country-and-western music and folk music. It is also popular as a children's toy.

Put a check (✓) next to the correct answers in the answer column.

Question	Answer
1. A summary of this research should	___ explain how the mouth organ works. ___ describe the mouth organ. ___ say that the modern instrument was invented in 1820.

2. Which of these best summarizes this research?	____ **Summary 1** The modern mouth organ was invented in 1820, and is popular as a children's toy today. ____ **Summary 2** The modern mouth organ was invented in 1820 and is used today in country-and-western and folk music.

4.5 Answers to Questions

Answers to 4.1

Correct Answer	Explanation
1. the cost and functions of different microwave ovens	By researching the cost and functions of microwave ovens, you can decide which one is affordable and suits your needs.
2. an article comparing the costs and options of microwave ovens an article examining the cooking times of microwave ovens compared with regular ovens	These articles will help you find out the cost and options of different microwave ovens, and how much cooking time is saved by using a microwave oven instead of a regular oven.

3. How much do microwave ovens cost, and what options are available? How much time is saved by using a microwave oven instead of a regular oven?	These are good questions for your research to answer. You need to find out the cost and options of microwave ovens. You also want to know the time-saving capabilities of microwave ovens compared with regular ovens.

Answers to 4.2a

Correct Answer	Explanation
The introduction of the tabloid newspaper in the 20th century has been an attempt to capture more of the market.	This idea will help you answer your research questions. It tells you that a recent trend is the introduction of tabloid newspapers. When you read sources, you should write down ideas that can answer one or more of your research questions.

Answers to 4.2b

Correct Answer	Explanation
Butterflies seek nectar from flowering plants.	This note tells you a complete idea about what butterflies eat. This is an important idea in understanding the feeding habits of butterflies.

Answers to 4.3

Correct Answer	Explanation
1. Improve bus service.	This is one of the ideas that support the main message of this research project. It shows that one way the city transportation system can be improved is by improving bus service. In a map, ideas that support each other are connected by lines.

2. Increase frequency of buses.	"Increase frequency of buses" is an example of a way of improving the bus service. So, a line connects it to the box that says "Improve bus service."

Answers to 4.4

Correct Answer	Explanation
1. say that the modern instrument was invented in 1820.	This idea should be included in a summary because part of the purpose for this research was to find out when the mouth organ was invented. Good summaries contain the most important ideas from your research.
2. **Summary 2** The modern mouth organ was invented in 1820 and is used today in country-and-western and folk music.	This sentence summarizes the research. It tells when the mouth organ was invented and in what kind of music it is used. The actual research project will expand on these two major ideas.

Chapter **5**
Locating Information

Learn how to read and interpret graphs, bibliographies, catalogs, charts, maps, schedules, and tables.

5.1 Bar Graphs: Gas Prices, Job Growth

5.1.1 Gasoline Prices in Selected Countries

Bar graphs show how much or how many by the length of bars used. The bars on this graph are shown horizontally. This bar graph shows the price of premium gasoline in selected countries.

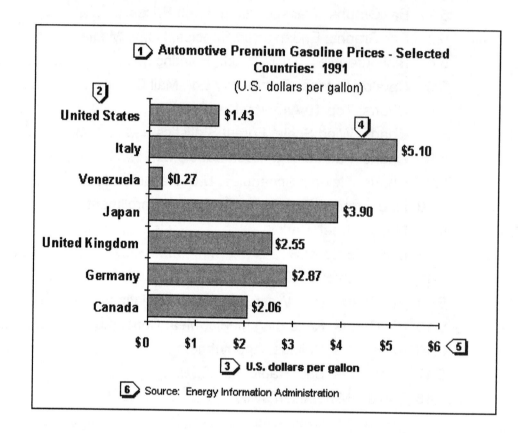

Understanding the Graph

To learn more about the graph, refer to the number labels on the graph and read the descriptions below.

1 ▷ title

The title gives a general idea about the graph's content. For example, this title says this graph will show the price, in U.S. dollars, of premium gasoline in selected countries in 1991.

2 ▷ countries

The names of the selected countries are listed here.

3 ▷ U.S. Dollars per gallon

This is a label. It tells you that the numbers listed across the bottom of the graph show the price of premium gasoline, in U.S. Dollars, in each country.

4 ▷ bar

Each bar shows the price of automotive premium gasoline in a specific country. The number at the end of the bar shows the price.

5 ▷ dollars

Each number across the bottom of the graph represents U.S. dollars. The numbers range from $0 to $6.

6 ▷ Source: Energy Information Administration

This is the source of the information shown in the graph.

Check Your Understanding 5.1.1

Refer to the this graph to answer the questions that follow. Put a check (✓) next to the correct answers in the answer column.

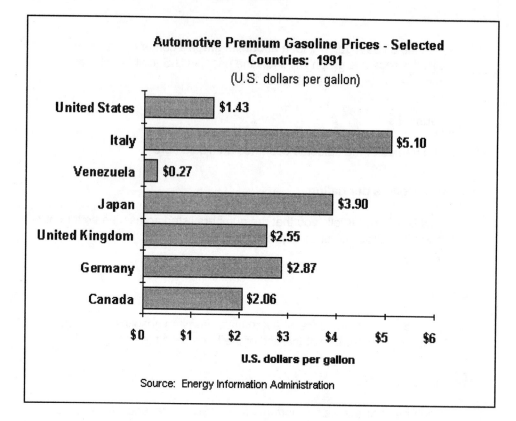

Question	Answer
1. What is the price per gallon of gasoline in Italy?	____ $1.43 ____ $0.27 ____ $2.87 ____ $5.10
2. According to the graph, in which country is gasoline about $4 per gallon?	____ Germany ____ Japan ____ United States ____ Canada
3. According to the graph, in which country is the price of gasoline the closest to the price in the U.S.?	____ Japan ____ United Kingdom ____ Germany ____ Canada
4. Based on what you see in the graph, which two countries have the closest gasoline prices?	____ United States and Canada ____ Germany and Canada ____ United Kingdom and Germany
5. A group of students plan to share the costs of renting a car during their vacation. In which country would their gasoline costs per gallon be the lowest?	____ Italy ____ Japan ____ United Kingdom ____ Germany
6. Countries that produce most or all of their own petroleum have cheaper gasoline prices than countries that do not produce most or all of their own petroleum. If this is true, which country on the graph would you say probably produces all or most of its own petroleum?	____ United States ____ Venezuela ____ Japan

5.1.2 Forecast of Job Growth in 10 Occupations

This bar graph shows the percentage change in the number of people employed in the 10 fastest growing occupations between 1992 and 2005.

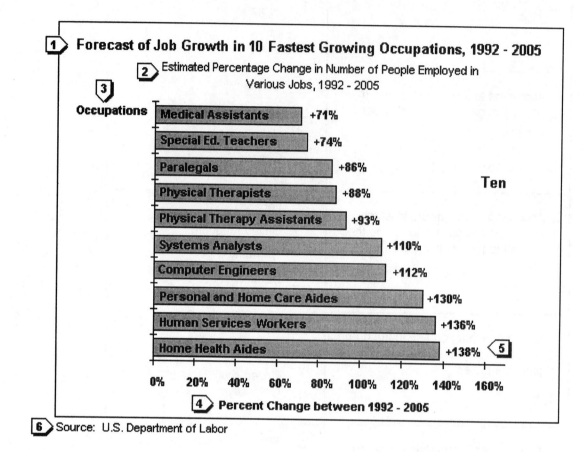

Forecast of Job Growth in 10 Fastest Growing Occupations, 1992 - 2005

Estimated Percentage Change in Number of People Employed in Various Jobs, 1992 - 2005

Occupations

Occupation	Percent Change
Medical Assistants	+71%
Special Ed. Teachers	+74%
Paralegals	+86%
Physical Therapists	+88%
Physical Therapy Assistants	+93%
Systems Analysts	+110%
Computer Engineers	+112%
Personal and Home Care Aides	+130%
Human Services Workers	+136%
Home Health Aides	+138%

Ten

Percent Change between 1992 - 2005

Source: U.S. Department of Labor

Understanding the Graph

To learn more about the graph, refer to the number labels on the graph and read the descriptions below.

1▷ title

The title gives a general idea about the graph's subject. For example, this title says this graph will show the predicted job growth in the 10 fastest growing occupations between 1992 and 2005.

2▷ subtitle

Subtitles provide details that can help you read a graph. This subtitle tells you that this graph shows the estimated percentage change in the number of people employed in various jobs between 1992 and 2005.

3▷ Occupations

The names of the 10 fastest growing occupations are listed here.

4▷ Percent Change between 1992 - 2005

This is a label. It tells you that the numbers listed across the bottom of the graph show the percent growth in each occupation between 1992 and 2005.

5▷ bar

Each bar shows the estimated percentage change in growth in a specific occupation. The number next to the bar shows the estimated percentage change.

6▷ Source: U.S. Department of Labor

This is the source of the information shown in the graph.

 **Check Your Understanding 5.1.2**

Refer to this graph to answer the questions that follow. Put a check (✓) next to the correct answers in the answer column.

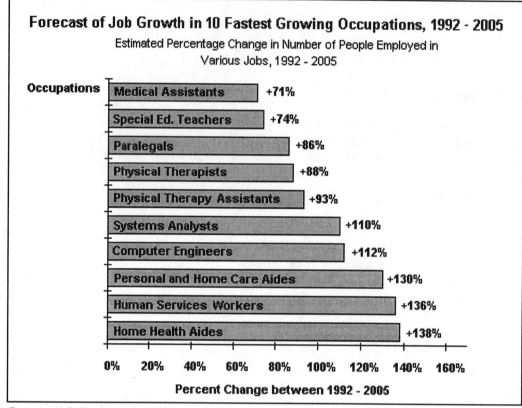

Forecast of Job Growth in 10 Fastest Growing Occupations, 1992 - 2005

Estimated Percentage Change in Number of People Employed in Various Jobs, 1992 - 2005

Occupations

Occupation	
Medical Assistants	+71%
Special Ed. Teachers	+74%
Paralegals	+86%
Physical Therapists	+88%
Physical Therapy Assistants	+93%
Systems Analysts	+110%
Computer Engineers	+112%
Personal and Home Care Aides	+130%
Human Services Workers	+136%
Home Health Aides	+138%

0%   20%   40%   60%   80%   100%   120%   140%   160%

Percent Change between 1992 - 2005

Source: U.S. Department of Labor

Question	Answer
1. According to the graph, what is the forecast percent growth for physical therapist jobs between 1992 and 2005?	___ 86% ___ 88% ___ 93%
2. According to the graph, which occupation is forecast to grow by 112% between 1992 and 2005?	___ Systems Analysts ___ Medical Assistants ___ Computer Engineers
3. If you were going into the legal profession as a paralegal, what percent increase in jobs could you expect in the next ten years?	___ 71% ___ 74% ___ 86%
4. According to the graph, which field is likely to have the greatest number of different jobs that will grow in the next ten years?	___ Teaching ___ Computers ___ Medicine/Health Care
5. Olivia is interested in computers. What percent growth could she expect in the number of people hired as systems analysts?	___ 74% ___ 110% ___ 130 %
6. Charles is making decisions about a career. If he wants a career in health care that is likely to have the most job opportunities in the future, which occupation should he consider?	___ Physical Therapy Assistant ___ Physical Therapist ___ Home Health Aide ___ Medical Assistant

5.2 Bar Graphs: Transportation, Food Prices

5.2.1 Changes in How Americans Get to Work

This type of bar graph uses the direction of the bars to show an increase or a decrease. Bars that appear above the horizontal line show an increase. Bars that appear below the line show a decrease. The length of the bars show how much of an increase or decrease. This bar graph shows how Americans have changed the form of transportation they use to get to work.

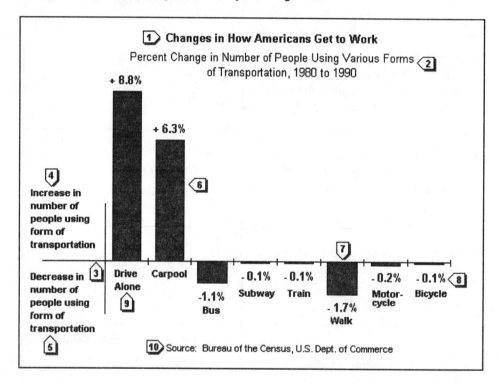

Understanding the Graph

To learn more about the graph above, refer to the number labels on the graph and read the descriptions below.

 title

The title gives a general idea about the graph's content. The title of this graph says the graph will show how Americans have changed the way they get to work.

2> **subtitle**

Subtitles provide details that can help you read a graph. This subtitle tells you that this graph shows changes in how Americans get to work from 1980 to 1990. The graph uses percentages to show whether the number of people using various forms of transportation, such as carpooling, increased or decreased.

3> **axis**

The axis, or horizontal line, represents zero--no change in the number of people using a form of transportation.

4> **Increase in number of people using a form of transportation**

This heading lets you know that bars above the axis show an increase in the number of people using a form of transportation.

5> **Decrease in number of people using a form of transportation**

This heading lets you know that bars below the axis show a decrease in the number of people using a form of transportation.

6> **bar that shows a positive change**

Each bar above the axis, or horizontal line, shows an increase in the number of people using a particular form of transportation.

7> **bar that shows a negative change**

Each bar below the axis, or horizontal line, shows a decrease in the number of people using a particular form of transportation.

8> **percent**

This is a percent. A plus (+) or a minus (-) sign appears before each percent on the graph. A positive percent (+) shows an increases in the use of a particular form of transportation, while a negative percent (-) shows a decrease in the use of a particular form of transportation.

9> **name of a form of transportation**

This is the name of a transportation form. For instance, the category *Walk* includes all the people who walk to work.

10> **Source: U.S. Department of Commerce**

This is the source of the information shown in the graph.

Check Your Understanding 5.2.1

Refer to this graph to answer the questions that follow. Put a check (✓) next to the correct answers in the answer column.

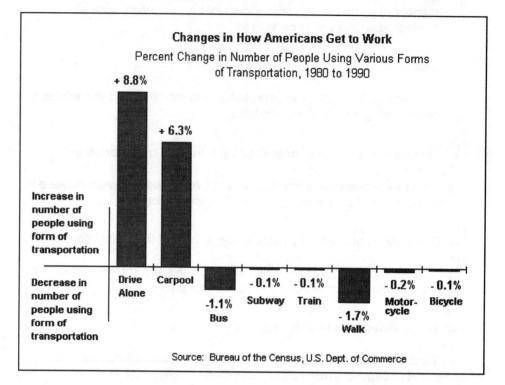

Question	Answer
1. According to this graph, the use of which forms of transportation changed the least?	____ bus, subway, and train ____ bicycle, subway, and train ____ motorcycle, train, and walk ____ walk, motorcycle, and bus
2. According to this graph, the number of people riding the bus to work decreased by	____ 0.1% ____ 1.1% ____ 1.7%

3. What assumptions must you make in order to interpret this graph? (Mark all that apply.)	___ Positive percents show increases; negative percents show decreases. ___ The bars represent total numbers of people using each form of transportation. ___ The longest bar shows the greatest % change; the shortest bar shows the least % change.
4. What conclusion should you NOT make when interpreting this graph?	___ The number of people carpooling to work has increased by 6.3%. ___ The number of people riding the train decreased by 0.1% in 1980. ___ The bicycle bar indicates a 0.1% decrease in the number of people riding bikes to work.
5. The Public Transportation Association wants to know if people used more or less public transportation during the 1980s. What do you tell them?	___ more ___ less
6. A commission studying the environment wants to know if an ad campaign they sponsored during the '80s had any effect. The ad campaign encouraged people to carpool or take public transportation instead of driving alone to work. Has driving alone to work decreased?	___ Yes ___ No

5.2.2 Changes in U.S. Food Retail Prices

This bar graph shows how U.S. retail prices of certain food items have changed between 1986 and 1992.

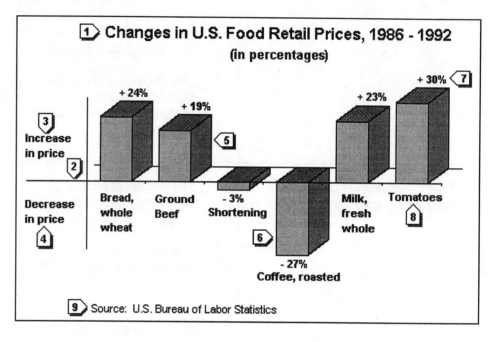

Understanding the Graph

To learn more about the graph, refer to the number labels on the graph and read the descriptions below.

1 ▷ title

The title gives a general idea about the graph's content. The title of this graph says the graph will show the changes in U.S. food retail prices (shown in percentages) between 1986 and 1992.

2 ▷ axis

The axis, or horizontal line, represents zero--no change in the price of a food item.

3 ▷ Increase in price

This heading lets you know that bars above the axis show an increase in price.

4 ▷ Decrease in price

This heading lets you know that bars below the axis show a decrease in price.

5 ▷ bar that shows a positive change

Each bar above the axis shows an increase in price.

6 ▷ bar that shows a negative change

Each bar below the axis shows a decrease in price.

7 ▷ percent

This is a percent. A plus (+) or a minus (-) sign appears before each percent on the graph. Positive percents (+) show increases in price, while negative percents (-) show decreases in price.

8 ▷ name of a food item

This is the name of a food item--for example, ground beef.

9 ▷ Source: U.S. Bureau of Labor Statistics

This is the source of the information shown in the graph.

 **Check Your Understanding 5.2.2**

Refer to this graph to answer the questions that follow. Put a check (✓) next to the correct answers in the answer column.

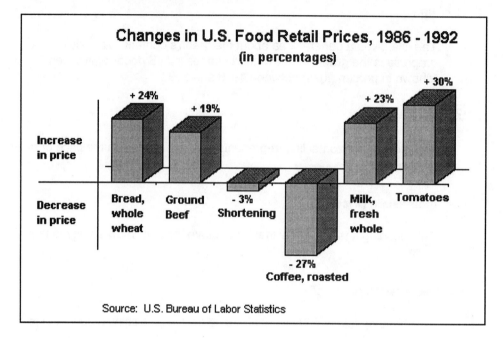

Question	Answer
1. According to this graph, which of these food items had the greatest percentage price change?	___ bread, whole wheat ___ coffee, roasted ___ ground beef ___ milk, fresh whole
2. According to this graph, the price of tomatoes increased by	___ 23% ___ 30% ___ 130%

3. What assumptions must you make in order to interpret this graph? (Mark all that apply.)	___ The axis (horizontal line) represents no change in the price. ___ The bars below the axis show a decrease in price; bars above the axis show an increase in price. ___ The bars represent the actual prices.
4. What conclusion should you NOT make when interpreting this graph?	___ The price of fresh whole milk has increased by 23%. ___ The *Bread, whole wheat* bar represents a 24% increase in price. ___ The price of coffee increased by 27%.
5. Celia is on a tight budget. Which food item could she get cheaper in the past than she can now?	___ shortening ___ coffee, roasted ___ bread, whole wheat
6. If the price of ground beef changes over the next six years as much as it did between 1986-1992, the manager of "Quick Burger" should plan to increase her prices for hamburgers by a minimum of what amount?	___ 19% ___ 24% ___ 30%

5.3 Bar Graphs: Endangered Species, Home Media

5.3.1 Endangered and Threatened Plants and Animals

This is a double bar graph that shows how many species of plants and animals were classified as endangered or threatened in 1992.

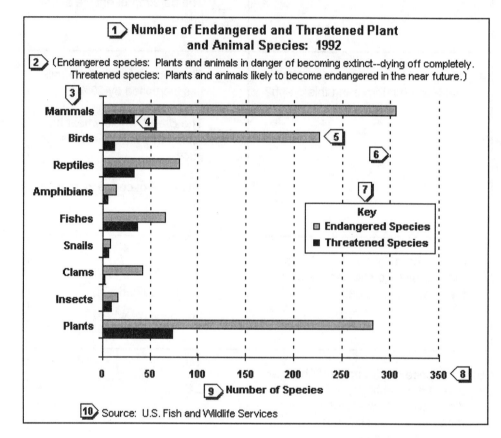

Number of Endangered and Threatened Plant and Animal Species: 1992

(Endangered species: Plants and animals in danger of becoming extinct--dying off completely. Threatened species: Plants and animals likely to become endangered in the near future.)

Source: U.S. Fish and Wildlife Services

Understanding the Graph

To learn more about the graph above, refer to the number labels on the graph and read the descriptions below.

 title

> The title gives a general idea about the graph's content. The title of this graph says the graph will show the number of endangered and threatened plant and animal species in 1992.

2▷ **subtitle definitions**

These definitions provide details that can help you read a graph. The definitions explain the difference between an endangered species and a threatened species.

3▷ **types of animals and plants**

The types (classes) of animals and plants (all plants are included under the *Plants* category) are listed down the side of the graph.

4▷ **Threatened Species bar**

This bar (■) represents threatened species in 1992. It shows how many plant and animal species were likely to become endangered in the near future. Longer bars indicate higher numbers of threatened species, while shorter bars show fewer threatened species.

5▷ **Endangered Species bar**

This bar (▨) represents endangered species in 1992. It shows how many plant and animal species were in danger of dying off. Longer bars indicate higher numbers of endangered species, while shorter bars show fewer endangered species.

6▷ **grid line**

These lines are used to extend the values shown on the scale at the bottom of the graph. They help you tell how far the bars reach.

7▷ **key**

The key explains which kind of bar represents Endangered Species (▨) and which represents Threatened Species (■).

8▷ **plant and animal species**

The numbers across the bottom of the graph represent species. The numbers range from 0 to 350.

9▷ **Number of Species**

This is a label. It tells you that the numbers listed across the bottom of the graph show the number of species.

10▷ **Source: U.S. Fish and Wildlife Service**

This is the source of the information shown in the graph.

 **Check Your Understanding 5.3.1**

Refer to this graph to answer the questions that follow. Put a check (✓) next to the correct answers in the answer column.

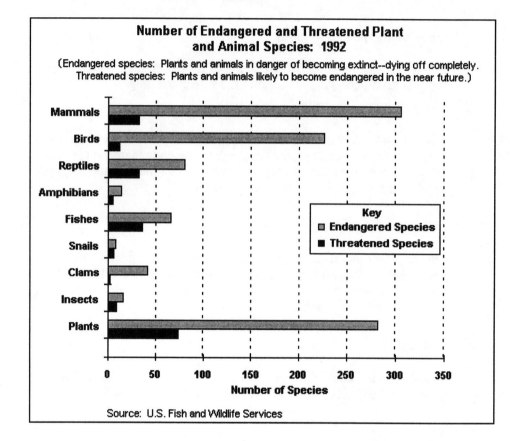

Question	Answer
1. According to the graph, approximately how many species of birds are classified as endangered?	___ 275 ___ 300 ___ 230 ___ 200
2. According to the graph, which category has the greatest number of threatened species?	___ Mammals ___ Plants ___ Birds ___ Reptiles
3. Finish this statement: There are ___ endangered birds species than mammal species.	___ more ___ fewer
4. Finish this statement: There are about ___ as many endangered clam species as endangered insect species.	___ twice ___ three times ___ four times
5. A school class plans to write letters to local businesses to ask for help in preserving the world's forests. How many plant species can they say are endangered?	___ almost 200 ___ almost 300 ___ almost 400
6. A team at the Cincinnati Zoo plans to preserve endangered species by reproducing animals in captivity. How many different species of reptiles do they need to be concerned about?	___ 50 ___ 75 ___ 100

5.3.2 Households With Selected Media

Bar graphs show how much or how many by the length of the bars used. This bar graph shows the percent of households in Culverton City that have selected media.

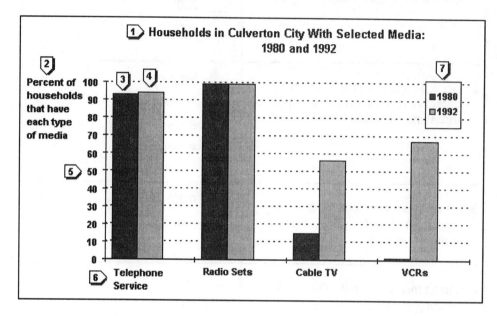

Understanding the Graph

To learn more about the graph, refer to the number labels on the graph and read the descriptions below.

1 title

The title gives a general idea about the graph's content. For example, this title says this graph will show Culverton City households that have selected media in 1980 and 1992.

2 Percent of households that have each type of media

This is a label. It tells you that the numbers listed down the side of the graph show what percent of the households have each type of media.

3 1980 bar

This bar (■) represents 1980. It shows what percentage of each type of media was in each Culverton City household in 1980. Longer bars indicate more households with a particular type of media, while shorter bars show fewer households.

4 1992 bar

This bar (▢) represents 1992. It shows what percentage of each type of media was in each Culverton City household in 1992. Longer bars indicate more households with a particular type of media, while shorter bars show fewer households.

5 percent

This is a percent. Each bar on the graph shows what percent of Culverton City households had selected media in 1980 and 1992. To find out what percent each bar represents, find the end of the bar, then look across at these percents. When a bar falls between two percents, you will have to estimate your answer.

6 types of media

Each category across the bottom of the graph represents the following types of media: telephone service, radio sets, cable TV, and VCRs.

7 key

The key explains which kind of bar represents 1980 (■) and which represents 1992 (▢).

Check Your Understanding 5.3.2

Refer to this graph to answer the questions that follow. Put a check (✓) next to the correct answers in the answer column.

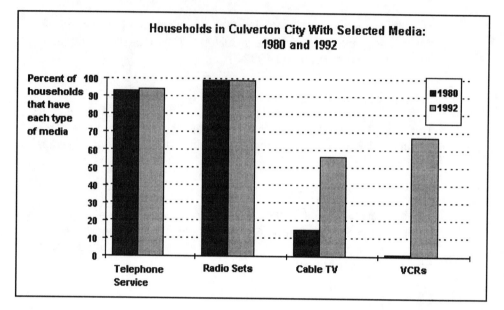

Question	Answer
1. According to the graph, which type of media was found in the most households in 1980?	___ telephone service ___ radio sets ___ cable TV ___ VCRs
2. According to the graph, which media showed the largest percent change between 1980 and 1992?	___ telephone service ___ radio sets ___ cable TV ___ VCRs
3. Based on what you learn from the graph, approximately what percent of the households had VCRs in 1992?	___ 50% ___ 60% ___ 70%
4. Finish this statement: By 1992 there were about ___ times as many households with cable TV as in 1980.	___ 4 ___ 6 ___ 8
5. A PTA group wants to conduct a telephone survey to find out what people in the community think about building a swimming pool on a school site. What percent of the households in the community would they be able to reach by phone based on the 1992 data?	___ around 80% ___ around 90% ___ around 100%
6. The Culverton City Council will begin charging a tax on cable TV use. What percent of the households would be required to pay this tax in 1992?	___ over 20% ___ almost 60% ___ almost 80%

5.4 Bibliographies: Social Work, Painting

5.4.1 Bibliographies: Social Work in the Twentieth Century

People who write research papers often include a bibliography at the end. A bibliography lists all written sources mentioned in the paper, such as books, magazines or journals. This bibliography gives the sources used in a research paper entitled "Social Work in the Twentieth Century." Bibliographies can follow different styles.

---

1 ▷ **BIBLIOGRAPHY for "Social Work in the Twentieth Century"**

6

Alpenstein, Garth and others. "Health Problems of Homeless Children in New York City." *American Journal of Public Health*, Sept. 1988.

7

Boyd, Nancy. *Emissaries: The Overseas Work of the American YWCA, 1985 - 1970,* Women's Press, 1987.

2 **3**

Ellwood, David T. *Poor Support: Poverty in the American Family,* Basic, 1988.

4 **5**

Fink, Arthur E. and others. *The Field of Social Work,* Sage, 8th ed., 1985.

Gilbo, Patrick F. *The American Red Cross: The First Century,* Harper, 1981.

Kozol, Jonathan. *Rachel and Her Children: Homeless Families in America,* Crown, 1988.

Riis, Jacob. *How the Other Half Lives*, Hill and Wang, 1957.

8

Simonsen, Clifford E. *Juvenile Justice in America*, Macmillan, 3rd ed., 1991.

Understanding the Bibliography

To learn more about the bibliography, refer to the number labels on the bibliography and read the following descriptions.

1 **title**

This title says that this is a bibliography and gives the name of the research paper.

2 **author's name**

In a bibliography entry for a book, magazine, or journal article, the author's name always comes first. The correct order in this style is last name, then comma, then first name.

3 **book title**

This is a book title. In this style of bibliography, book titles are in italics and appear after the author's name.

4 **publishing company**

This is the name of a book publisher. This information would help you find this book in a bookstore or library.

5 **publication date**

In a bibliography entry, the year a book was published (or the date a magazine issue was published) is written after the name of the publisher.

6 **article title**

This is the title of an article that appeared in a journal called *American Journal of Public Health*. Article titles are put in quotation marks.

7 **journal title**

American Journal of Public Health is the title of a health journal. In this style, journal titles are in italics.

8 **ed.**

This is an edition of a book. For example, 3rd ed. means that this is the third edition of this book.

 **Check Your Understanding 5.4.1**

Refer to this bibliography to answer the questions that follow. Put a check (✓) next to the correct answers in the answer column.

BIBLIOGRAPHY for "Social Work in the Twentieth Century"

Alpenstein, Garth and others. "Health Problems of Homeless Children in New York City." *American Journal of Public Health*, Sept. 1988.

Boyd, Nancy. *Emissaries: The Overseas Work of the American YWCA, 1985 - 1970,* Women's Press, 1987.

Ellwood, David T. *Poor Support: Poverty in the American Family,* Basic, 1988.

Fink, Arthur E. and others. *The Field of Social Work,* Sage, 8th ed., 1985.

Gilbo, Patrick F. *The American Red Cross: The First Century,* Harper, 1981.

Kozol, Jonathan. *Rachel and Her Children: Homeless Families in America,* Crown, 1988.

Riis, Jacob. *How the Other Half Lives,* Hill and Wang, 1957.

Simonsen, Clifford E. *Juvenile Justice in America,* Macmillan, 3rd ed., 1991.

Question	Answer
1. According to this bibliography, *The Field of Social Work* was published in	____ 1981 ____ 1985 ____ 1987 ____ 1988
2. Who was the author of the only journal article in this bibliography?	____ David Ellwood ____ Jacob Riis ____ Garth Alpenstein and others ____ Nancy Boyd
3. Which source has been printed in the most editions?	____ *Juvenile Justice in America* ____ *The Field of Social Work* ____ *How the Other Half Lives*
4. What company published *The American Red Cross: The First Century*?	____ Harper ____ Hill and Wang ____ Macmillan
5. Which source is the most recent listed in the bibliography?	____ *Poor Support: Poverty in the American Family* ____ *How the Other Half Lives* ____ *Juvenile Justice in America*
6. A class is interested in learning more about homeless children. Which authors' sources would be useful? (Mark all that apply.)	____ Alpenstein, Garth and others ____ Gilbo, Patrick F. ____ Kozol, Jonathan

5.4.2 Bibliographies: Painting in Watercolors

This bibliography gives the sources used in a research paper entitled "Painting in Watercolors." Bibliographies can follow different styles. This bibliography follows a style commonly used for scholarly works in literature and the arts.

---

[1] BIBLIOGRAPHY for "Painting in Watercolors"

[2]   [3]   [4]

Crespo, Michael. *Watercolor Day by Day.* New York: Watson-Guptill, 1987.

[5]

Gaunt, William. *The March of the Moderns.* New York: Hyperion, 1979.

Griffith, Thomas. *A Practical Guide for Beginning Painters.* Englewood Cliffs, New Jersey: Prentice Hall, 1981.

Reid, Charles. *Figure Painting in Watercolors.* New York: Watson-Guptill, 1976.

Taubes, Frederic. *The Painter's Dictionary of Materials and Methods.* New York: Watson-Guptill, 1979.

Whitney, Edgar A. *A Complete Guide to Watercolor Painting.* New York: Watson-Guptill, 1972.

Understanding the Bibliography

To learn more about the bibliography, refer to the number labels on the bibliography and read the descriptions below.

1 **title**

This title says that this is a bibliography and gives the name of the research paper.

2 **author's name**

In a bibliography entry for a book, magazine, or journal article, the author's name always comes first. The correct order in this style is last name, then comma, then first name.

3 **book title**

This is a book title. In this style of bibliography, book titles are italicized and appear after the author's name.

4 **publishing information**

This is the name of a book publisher and the town where it was published. This information would help you find this book in a bookstore or library. In this style, the correct order is town, then colon (:), and then publishing company.

5 **publication date**

In a bibliography entry, the year a book was published (or the date a magazine issue was published) is written after the name of the publisher.

Check Your Understanding 5.4.2

Refer to this bibliography to answer the questions that follow. Put a check (✓) next to the correct answers in the answer column.

BIBLIOGRAPHY for "Painting in Watercolors"

Crespo, Michael. *Watercolor Day by Day.* New York: Watson-Guptill, 1987.

Gaunt, William. *The March of the Moderns.* New York: Hyperion, 1979.

Griffith, Thomas. *A Practical Guide for Beginning Painters.* Englewood Cliffs, New Jersey: Prentice-Hall, 1981.

Reid, Charles. *Figure Painting in Watercolors.* New York: Watson-Guptill, 1976.

Taubes, Frederic. *The Painter's Dictionary of Materials and Methods.* New York: Watson-Guptill, 1979.

Whitney, Edgar A. *A Complete Guide to Watercolor Painting.* New York: Watson-Guptill, 1972.

Question	Answer
1. Where was *Figure Painting in Watercolors* published?	___ New York ___ Englewood Cliffs ___ New Jersey
2. What company published *A Complete Guide to Watercolor Painting*?	___ Whitney ___ Watson-Guptill ___ Prentice-Hall ___ Edgar
3. If you wanted to inquire about buying *A Practical Guide for Beginning Painters*, who would you call?	___ Watson Guptill, New York City ___ Hyperion, New York City ___ Prentice Hall, Englewood Cliffs, New Jersey
4. Which is the most recent source listed in this bibliography?	___ *Watercolor Day by Day* ___ *The March of the Moderns* ___ *A Practical Guide for Beginning Painters*
5. Which author's source would you turn to if you wanted to quickly look up terms related to painting?	___ Crespo ___ Gaunt ___ Taubes
6. If you wanted to learn more about modern watercolor painters, which author's work would you refer to?	___ Gaunt ___ Griffith ___ Taubes

5.5 Catalog Entries: Community Ed., Mail Order

5.5.1 Beginning Video Class

Catalog entries are organized to make it easy for readers to find information. This entry from a college catalog gives students information about a video production class.

1▷ *BEGINNING VIDEO*

2▷ Art 300R-43 (4 hours credit, tuition + $40 special fee) ◁3

4▷ W 7:15-10:15 p.m., Feb. 28-May 1.

5▷ Additional lab hours arranged.

6▷ SPRINGDALE FILM AND VIDEO CENTER
21 Oak St.
8▽
C. Wilkinson ◁7

This is an introductory course in video production. Students learn the fundamentals of filming videos from an artistic point of view as well as a technical point of view, including preproduction, shooting, and editing.

Understanding the Catalog Entry

To learn more about the catalog entry, refer to the number labels on the catalog entry and read the descriptions below.

1 **title**

The title tells you what the catalog entry is about generally. In this case, the title lets you know that the entry is about a course called "Beginning Video."

2 **Art 300R-43**

This line tells you that this is a required (R) 300 level class in the art department. This catalog entry describes section 43 of the class. Another section of the class (section 42) might be offered at a different time.

3 **(4 hours credit, tuition + $40 special fee)**

This line tells you how many credits the class is worth, and how much money it costs to take the class.

4 **W 7:15-10:15 p.m., Feb. 28-May 1.**

This line tells you the class is held on Wednesdays from 7:15 to 10:15 p.m. The class starts on February 28th and ends on May 1st.

5 **Additional lab hours arranged**

This line tells you that a lab will be held in addition to the time the class meets.

6 **SPRINGDALE FILM AND VIDEO CENTER**
21 Oak St.

The line tells where the class is held.

7 **C. Wilkinson**

This line tells you that C. Wilkinson is the teacher for this video class.

8 **course description**

This is the course description. This paragraph describes the topics covered in the course.

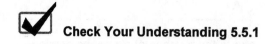 **Check Your Understanding 5.5.1**

Refer to this catalog entry to answer the questions that follow. Put a check (✓) next to the correct answers in the answer column.

BEGINNING VIDEO

Art 300R-43 (4 hours credit, tuition + $40 special fee)

W 7:15-10:15 p.m., Feb. 28-May 1.

Additional lab hours arranged.

SPRINGDALE FILM AND VIDEO CENTER
21 Oak St.
C. Wilkinson

This is an introductory course in video production. Students learn the fundamentals of filming videos from an artistic point of view as well as a technical point of view, including preproduction, shooting, and editing.

Question	Answer
1. On which day is this course held?	___ Mondays ___ Tuesdays ___ Wednesdays ___ Thursdays
2. How many hours of credit is this course worth?	___ 43 ___ 4 ___ 40 ___ 3
3. How much will you have to pay to take this class in addition to paying tuition?	___ nothing ___ $20 ___ $40
4. What if you've had no prior experience shooting video? Is it okay for you to take this class?	___ Yes ___ No
5. Which of these topics will probably NOT be covered in this course?	___ preproduction ___ shooting ___ editing ___ creating special effects
6. If you planned on attending all of the classes, approximately how many times would you attend the class?	___ 6 ___ 10 ___ 15

5.5.2 Magnetic Photo Album

Catalog entries are organized to make it easy for readers to find information. This entry from a mail-order catalog gives information about a photo album.

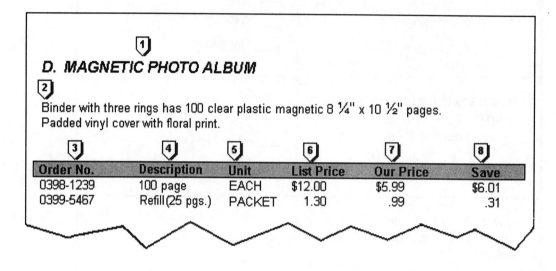

Understanding the Catalog Entry

To learn more about the catalog entry, refer to the number labels on the catalog entry and read the descriptions below.

1 **title**

The title tells you what the catalog entry is about generally. In this case, the title lets you know that the entry is for a "Magnetic Photo Album." The D refers to the label shown on a picture of the photo album on another page.

2 **item description**

This is the item description. This paragraph describes the photo album.

3 **Order No.**

This column tells you the order numbers of the photo album and the refill.

4 **Description**

This column tells you that the photo album is 100 pages and that a refill with 25 pages per packet is also available.

5 **Unit**

This column tells the unit the price applies to. For instance, the price listed for the refill applies to the whole packet of 25 pages, not to each page in the packet.

6 **List Price**

This column gives the list price of each item. The list price is the manufacturer's suggested retail price. The catalog uses the list price as a comparison for the price the catalog company is able to offer.

7 **Our Price**

This column gives the price the catalog company is charging for each item.

8 **Save**

The column shows the difference between the List Price and Our Price. In other words, the amount the customer saves.

Check Your Understanding 5.5.2

Refer to this catalog entry to answer the questions that follow. Put a check (✓) next to the correct answers in the answer column.

D. MAGNETIC PHOTO ALBUM

Binder with three rings has 100 clear plastic magnetic 8 ¼" x 10 ½" pages.
Padded vinyl cover with floral print.

Order No.	Description	Unit	List Price	Our Price	Save
0398-1239	100 page	EACH	$12.00	$5.99	$6.01
0399-5467	Refill (25 pgs.)	PACKET	1.30	.99	.31

Question	Answer
1. What is the list price for the 100-page photo album?	___ $12.00 ___ $5.99 ___ $6.01 ___ $1.29
2. How much does a customer save when a refill is purchased from this company?	___ $1.60 ___ $1.29 ___ $6.01 ___ $0.31
3. Denten wants to order the album. Which order number should he write on the order form?	___ 0399-5467 ___ 0398-1239
4. Phuong wants a leather photo album with plastic magnetic pages, should she buy this album?	___ Yes ___ No

5. How many refills would you need to buy to double the number of pages in your album?	___ 2 ___ 3 ___ 4
6. Approximately how much would it cost to order the album and one refill from this company?	___ $6.00 ___ $7.00 ___ $8.00

5.6 Charts: Top 10 Airports, Distances

Charts often organize information into columns and rows. **Columns** go up and down a chart like this:

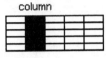

Rows go across a chart like this:

Each of the boxes formed where rows and columns come together are called **cells**. Often you will need to locate information in a chart by searching for specific row and column headings and then following along the row and column until you find the particular information you need in the cell.

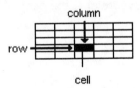

Other times you will search for information using the opposite strategy. You will see the information that interests you in a particular cell and then you will need to follow along the row and column to see the headings for the categories this cell fits under.

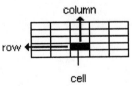

Now you are ready to practice reading different kinds of charts.

145

5.6.1 Top 10 Airports in U.S. — Traffic Summary

This chart shows a traffic summary of the 10 busiest airports in the United States.

1 ⊳Top 10 Airports in U.S. — Traffic Summary: 1991

2 ⊳Airports ranked by paying passengers boarding at airport, 1991.

3	4	5	6
AIRPORT	**RANK**	**AIRCRAFT DEPARTURES** **(In thousands)**	**PAYING PASSENGERS BOARDING** **(In thousands)**
Atlanta, Hartsfield International	4	206	17,691
Chicago, O'Hare	1	329	25,872
Dallas/Ft. Worth International	2	269	22,656
Denver, Stapleton International	6	151	12,314
Detroit, Metro Wayne	9	132	9,618
Los Angeles International	3	199	18,303
Newark International	8	128	9,737
Phoenix, Sky Harbor International	7	145	10,972
San Francisco International	5	168	14,026
St. Louis International	10	160	9,352

7 ⊳Source: U.S. Federal Aviation Administration and Research and Special Programs Administration

Understanding the Chart

To learn more about the chart above, refer to the number labels on the chart and read the descriptions below.

 title

The title gives a general idea about the chart's content. This title says the chart shows a traffic summary of the top 10 U.S. airports in 1991.

⟨2⟩ **subtitle**

The subtitle explains what the chart is about in more detail than the title. This subtitle says the chart has ranked airports by the number of paying passengers boarding at each airport.

⟨3⟩ **Airport**

The top 10 airports are listed in alphabetical order under this column heading.

⟨4⟩ **Rank**

This column lists the ranks of the airports from one to 10, according to how many paying passengers boarded planes at each airport in 1991. The airport that had the most boarding passengers is ranked in position 1, the airport that had the second most boarding passengers is in position 2, and so on.

⟨5⟩ **Aircraft Departures (In thousands)**

This column shows the number of aircraft that departed from each airport during 1991. The numbers are shown in thousands. This means you need to multiply each number shown by 1,000 (add three zeros to the end of each number) to get the actual number. For example, the number 206 on the chart represents 206,000 planes that departed from the airport at Atlanta, Hartsfield International.

⟨6⟩ **Paying Passengers Boarding (In thousands)**

This column shows the number of paying passengers that got on aircraft at each airport in 1991. The numbers are shown in thousands. This means you need to multiply each number shown by 1,000 (add three zeros to the end of each number) to get the actual number. For example, the number 9,618 on the chart represents 9,618,000 passengers.

⟨7⟩ **Source: U.S. Federal Aviation Administration and Research and Special Programs Administration**

This note tells you the source of the figures used in this chart.

 **Check Your Understanding 5.6.1**

Refer to this chart to answer the questions that follow. Put a check (✓) next to the correct answers in the answer column.

Top 10 Airports in U.S. — Traffic Summary: 1991

Airports ranked by paying passengers boarding at airport, 1991.

AIRPORT	RANK	AIRCRAFT DEPARTURES (In thousands)	PAYING PASSENGERS BOARDING (In thousands)
Atlanta, Hartsfield International	4	206	17,691
Chicago, O'Hare	1	329	25,872
Dallas/Ft. Worth International	2	269	22,656
Denver, Stapleton International	6	151	12,314
Detroit, Metro Wayne	9	132	9,618
Los Angeles International	3	199	18,303
Newark International	8	128	9,737
Phoenix, Sky Harbor International	7	145	10,972
San Francisco International	5	168	14,026
St. Louis International	10	160	9,352

Source: U.S. Federal Aviation Administration and Research and Special Programs Administration

Question	Answer
1. Based on the number of paying passengers boarding at an airport, the third busiest airport in 1991 was	___ Chicago, O'Hare ___ Dallas/Ft. Worth International ___ San Francisco International ___ Los Angeles International
2. How many paying passengers boarded aircraft at Newark International Airport in 1991?	___ 128,000 ___ 9,737 ___ 10,972,000 ___ 9,737,000
3. Which airport listed had the fewest number of aircraft departures in 1991?	___ St. Louis International ___ Denver, Stapleton International ___ Newark International ___ Detroit Metro Wayne
4. How many planes left from the Phoenix Sky Harbor International Airport in 1991?	___ 145 ___ 145,000 ___ 144,000,000
5. Finish this statement: To be listed as one of the top 10 airports in 1991, the airport had at least ___ passengers boarding at the airport.	___ 9,352 ___ 9,352,000 ___ 935,200,000
6. A travel agent tries to route his vacation travelers through less busy airports. Which airport should he try to avoid the most?	___ Atlanta, Hartsfield ___ Chicago, O'Hare ___ San Francisco International

5.6.2 Distances From Place to Place

Charts organize information in columns and rows. Columns go up and down a chart; rows run across a chart. This chart shows the distances between places.

1 Distances From Place to Place
(in miles)

	Darwin, Australia	London, England	Mexico City, Mexico	Moscow, Russia	New York, U.S.A.	Paris, France	Tokyo, Japan
Darwin, Australia	**5**	8595	9081	7046	9959	8575	3367
London, England	8598		5541	1549	3459	213	5938
Mexico City, Mexico	9081	5541 **4**		6688	2085	5706	7035
Moscow, Russia	7046	1549	6688		4662	1541	4650
New York, U.S.A.	9959	3459	2085	4662		3622	6733
Paris, France	8575	213	5706	1541	3622		6033
Tokyo, Japan	3367	5938	7035	4650	6735	6033	

Understanding the Chart

To learn more about the chart, refer to the number labels on the chart and read the descriptions below.

1 title

The title gives a general idea about the chart's contents. This title says that the chart shows distances between places.

2 column heading

Each column heading shows the name of a world city.

3 row heading

Each row heading shows the name of a world city.

4 number

This number is the distance, in miles, between London and Mexico City. You find this number by looking at the column heading for one of the cities and the row heading for the other city. Then draw an imaginary line from each heading till they meet in the box with the number 5541.

5 blank boxes

When the column heading and the row heading are the same city, the box at the end of the imaginary lines will be empty.

 **Check Your Understanding 5.6.2**

Refer to this chart to answer the questions that follow. Put a check (✓) next to the correct answers in the answer column.

Distances From Place to Place
(in miles)

	Darwin, Australia	London, England	Mexico City, Mexico	Moscow, Russia	New York, U.S.A.	Paris, France	Tokyo, Japan
Darwin, Australia		8595	9081	7046	9959	8575	3367
London, England	8598		5541	1549	3459	213	5938
Mexico City, Mexico	9081	5541		6688	2085	5706	7035
Moscow, Russia	7046	1549	6688		4662	1541	4650
New York, U.S.A.	9959	3459	2085	4662		3622	6733
Paris, France	8575	213	5706	1541	3622		6033
Tokyo, Japan	3367	5938	7035	4650	6735	6033	

Question	Answer
1. How far is it from Moscow to New York?	____ 4,650 miles ____ 1,541 miles ____ 6,688 miles ____ 4,662 miles
2. Which city is 6,033 miles from Paris?	____ Darwin ____ Mexico City ____ Tokyo ____ New York
3. Which city on the chart is the greatest distance from Darwin, Australia?	____ New York ____ London ____ Mexico City
4. The distance between Moscow and which two cities is almost the same?	____ New York Paris, France ____ Darwin, Australia London, England ____ New York Tokyo, Japan
5. Marcus won a plane trip to any place within 5,000 miles of New York City. Which cities can he choose to visit? (Mark all that apply.)	____ London, England ____ Tokyo, Japan ____ Moscow, Russia ____ Paris, France
6. Sara is planning a business trip that will take her from New York City to Mexico City and then on to London and back to New York City. Approximately how many miles will she travel?	____ 6,000 miles ____ 8,000 miles ____ 11,000 miles

5.7 Charts: Wind Scale, Forest Statistics

5.7.1 Beaufort Wind Scale

This chart shows a wind classification system based on wind speed. The Beaufort wind scale is used by sailors and weather forecasters to describe winds. Francis Beaufort, an Irish scientist, first came up with the scale in 1805. His original categories were later modified. Below is the current version of the scale.

This chart has column headings that show a numbered scale, a description of the wind at each level, the equivalent wind speed, and characteristics. Each level of the scale has its own row, even though there aren't any lines to show it.

1 **Beaufort Wind Scale**

2 Based on wind speed measured in miles per hour.

3   4   5   6

Number	Description	Speed (m.p.h.)	Characteristics
0	Calm	less than 1	Smoke rises vertically
1	Light air	1-3	Smoke drifts with air
2	Light breeze	4-7	Weather vanes active
3	Gentle breeze	8-12	Leaves and small twigs move
4	Moderate breeze	13-18	Small branches sway
5	Fresh breeze	19-24	Small trees sway
6	Strong breeze	25-31	Umbrellas difficult to use
7	Moderate gale	32-38	Difficult to walk against wind
8	Fresh gale	39-46	Twigs broken off trees
9	Strong gale	47-54	Shingles blown off roof
10	Whole gale	55-63	Trees uprooted; considerable damage
11	Storm	64-73	Widespread damage
12-17	Hurricane	74 and above	Violent destruction

Understanding the Chart

To learn more about the chart, refer to the number labels on the chart and read the descriptions below.

1 **title**

The title gives a general idea about the chart's contents. This title says that the chart shows a wind scale.

2 **subtitle**

The subtitle explains what the chart is about in more detail than the title. This subtitle says the chart is based on wind speed measured in miles per hour.

3 **Number**

This column includes a heading and, underneath the heading, the numbers of the wind scale.

4 **Description**

This column has a heading and, underneath the heading, descriptions of the wind for each number of the wind scale.

5 **Speed (m.p.h.)**

At the top of this column is a heading. Underneath the heading are the wind speeds related to each number on the wind scale.

6 **Characteristics**

This column has a heading at the top. Beneath the heading is a list of the characteristics, or effects of the wind, for each number on the wind scale.

Check Your Understanding 5.7.1

Refer to this chart to answer the questions that follow. Put a check (✓) next to the correct answers in the answer column.

Beaufort Wind Scale
Based on wind speed measured in miles per hour.

Number	Description	Speed (m.p.h.)	Characteristics
0	Calm	less than 1	Smoke rises vertically
1	Light air	1-3	Smoke drifts with air
2	Light breeze	4-7	Weather vanes active
3	Gentle breeze	8-12	Leaves and small twigs move
4	Moderate breeze	13-18	Small branches sway
5	Fresh breeze	19-24	Small trees sway
6	Strong breeze	25-31	Umbrellas difficult to use
7	Moderate gale	32-38	Difficult to walk against wind
8	Fresh gale	39-46	Twigs broken off trees
9	Strong gale	47-54	Shingles blown off roof
10	Whole gale	55-63	Trees uprooted; considerable damage
11	Storm	64-73	Widespread damage
12-17	Hurricane	74 and above	Violent destruction

Question	Answer
1. What is the wind scale number of a moderate gale?	___ 7 ___ 8 ___ 9
2. What is the wind speed during a fresh breeze?	___ 13-18 miles per hour ___ 19-24 miles per hour ___ 39-46 miles per hour
3. What are the characteristics of a force 11 wind?	___ Small trees sway ___ Widespread damage ___ Violent destruction
4. Oriana has a new kite that flies best in 8-10 mph winds. The newspaper weather report says the Beaufort wind scale number will be about a level 1 tomorrow. Should she plan to fly her kite then?	___ Yes ___ No
5. Stuart usually takes his fishing boat back to the dock any time there are winds over 30 mph. He hears over the radio that a fresh gale will be blowing through later in the afternoon. Should he return to the dock?	___ Yes ___ No
6. Hector is buying some shutters for his house. The salesperson says the shutters are guaranteed to resist winds up to 50 miles per hour. Should Hector feel comfortable that these shutters will protect his windows in a hurricane?	___ Yes ___ No

5.7.2 Forest Statistics

This chart shows information about the forests of the world. Each type of forest has its own row. The columns show information about temperature, rainfall, and growing season.

1▷ **Forest Statistics**

2▷ Temperature, rainfall, and growing season differences among coniferous, deciduous, and rain forests.

3 Type of Forest	4 Average Temperature	5 Average Rainfall Per Year	6 Growing Season Length
Coniferous forest A forest that has evergreen trees with needle-like leaves.	High: 20°C Low: -30°C	25-125 cm	2-5 months
Deciduous forest A forest that has broadleaf trees that shed their leaves seasonally.	High: 27°C Low: -10°C	75-125 cm	6 months
Rain forest A tropical forest that has broadleaf, evergreen trees.	High: 35°C Low: 25°C	212 cm	9-12 months

Understanding the Chart

To learn more about the chart, refer to the number labels on the chart and read the descriptions below.

1 **title**

The title gives a general idea about the chart's contents. This title says that the chart shows forest statistics.

2 **subtitle**

The subtitle explains what the chart is about in more detail than the title. This subtitle says the chart shows temperature, rainfall, and growing season differences among coniferous, deciduous, and rain forests.

3 **Type of Forest**

This column has a heading and, underneath the heading, a brief description of each type of forest.

4 **Average Temperature**

This is a column heading. Underneath the heading, the average high and low temperatures for each type of forest are listed.

5 **Average Rainfall Per Year**

The average yearly rainfall for each type of forest is listed under this column heading.

6 **Growing Season Length**

This column has a heading at the top. Beneath the heading the length of the growing season in each type of forest is listed. The growing season is the optimum time for new plant growth, usually between the first frosts in the spring and fall.

 **Check Your Understanding 5.7.2**

Refer to this chart to answer the questions that follow. Put a check (✓) next to the correct answers in the answer column.

Forest Statistics

Temperature, rainfall, and growing season differences
among coniferous, deciduous, and rain forests.

Type of Forest	Average Temperature	Average Rainfall Per Year	Growing Season Length
Coniferous forest A forest that has evergreen trees with needle-like leaves.	High: 20°C Low: -30°C	25-125 cm	2-5 months
Deciduous forest A forest that has broadleaf trees that shed their leaves seasonally.	High: 27°C Low: -10°C	75-125 cm	6 months
Rain forest A tropical forest that has broadleaf, evergreen trees.	High: 35°C Low: 25°C	212 cm	9-12 months

Question	Answer
1. What is the average high temperature in a deciduous forest?	___ -10°C ___ 27°C ___ 35°C
2. What type of forest has a growing season length of 9-12 months?	___ coniferous forest ___ deciduous forest ___ rain forest
3. Which type of forest gets the least rain per year?	___ coniferous forest ___ deciduous forest ___ rain forest
4. The forests in Alaska have a short growing season (only several months). What type of forests grow in Alaska?	___ coniferous forests ___ deciduous forests ___ rain forests
5. The Black Forest is a wooded mountain region in Southwestern Germany. It is noted for the dark color of the fir trees on its upper slopes. The lower parts of this region are covered in dense forests of broadleaf oak and beech trees that shed their leaves seasonally. What would you expect the average yearly rainfall would be in these oak and beech forests?	___ 25-125 cm ___ 75-125 cm ___ 212 cm
6. Omar just bought a tropical plant from a nursery. To keep this plant alive, he should keep it in a place with what kind of temperature range?	___ -30°C to 20°C ___ -10°C to 27°C ___ 25°C to 35°C

5.8 Charts: Fundraising, Food Labels

5.8.1 Fund-raising Goals for the Animal Shelter

This chart shows the fund-raising goals that have been set to raise money for an animal shelter.

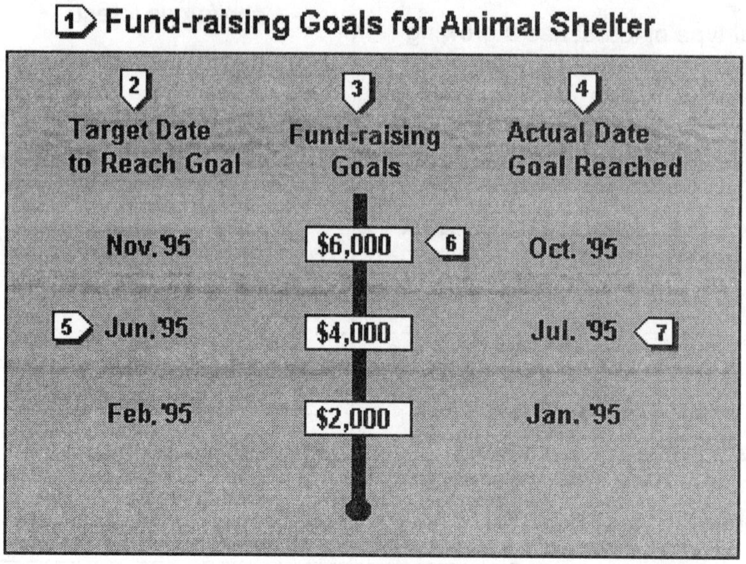

1 **Fund-raising Goals for Animal Shelter**

2 Target Date to Reach Goal	3 Fund-raising Goals	4 Actual Date Goal Reached
Nov. '95	$6,000 6	Oct. '95
5 Jun. '95	$4,000	Jul. '95 7
Feb. '95	$2,000	Jan. '95

Understanding the Chart

To learn more about the chart, refer to the number labels on the chart and read the descriptions below.

1▷ title

The title gives a general idea about the chart's contents. This title says that the chart shows fund-raising goals for an animal shelter.

2▷ Target Date to Reach Goal

This is a column heading with target dates listed under it. These are dates by which each financial goal is to be reached.

3▷ Fund-raising Goals

The financial goals appear under this column heading. The goals are arranged in ascending order, from the bottom to the top of the thermometer. The first goal is $2,000 and the end goal is $6,000.

4▷ Actual Date Goal Reached

Listed under this column heading are the actual dates when each financial goal was reached.

5▷ target date

This is a date by which the financial goal alongside it is to be reached. For example, the plan is to raise $4,000 by June 1995.

6▷ goal

This is a financial goal. The overall goal is to raise a total of $6,000.

7▷ actual date

This is the actual date that the financial goal alongside it was reached. For example, $4,000 was raised by July 1995.

Check Your Understanding 5.8.1

Refer to this chart to answer the questions that follow. Put a check (✓) next to the correct answers in the answer column.

Fund-raising Goals for Animal Shelter

Target Date to Reach Goal	Fund-raising Goals	Actual Date Goal Reached
Nov. '95	$6,000	Oct. '95
Jun. '95	$4,000	Jul. '95
Feb. '95	$2,000	Jan. '95

Question	Answer
1. What is the target date to raise $2,000?	___ Feb. '95 ___ Jan. '95 ___ Jun. '95
2. When was $6,000 raised?	___ Nov. '95 ___ Oct.' 95 ___ Jul. '95
3. How much money was raised between Jul. '95 and Oct. '95?	___ $2,000 ___ $4,000 ___ $6,000
4. How many months from the first goal date were planned to raise $6,000?	___ 10 months ___ 11 months ___ 12 months
5. How many months from the first goal date did it actually take to raise $6,000?	___ 10 months ___ 11 months ___ 12 months
6. The fund-raising committee is planning next year's drive. They want to base their new target dates on what actually happened last year. Which months should they choose as their target dates for reaching their $2,000, $4,000, and $6,000 goals?	___ Feb., Jun., Nov. ___ Jan., Jul., Oct. ___ Feb., Jun., Oct.

5.8.2 Food Labels

This chart shows an example of a food label with nutritional information. The Federal Nutrition Labeling and Education Act of 1990 established new guidelines for labeling food products. By 1994 all processed foods must have labels with a format similar to the one shown below. The main advantage to these new labels is that you should be able to believe the information they contain. Government regulations now standardize and regulate the use of the terms and claims on the labels.

1️⃣ **Food Labeling**

2️⃣ Nutritional information on the label of a 10 oz. package of chocolate mint cookies.

3️⃣

Nutrition Facts

Serving Size: 4 cookies (28g)
Servings Per Container: About 10

Amount Per Serving 4️⃣

Calories   150   Calories from Fat 70

5️⃣   6️⃣ **% Daily Value***

Total Fat 8g	12%
Saturated Fat 5g	25%
Cholesterol 0mg	0%
Sodium 70mg	3%
Total Carbohydrate 18g	6%
Dietary Fiber 0.5g	2%
Sugars 9g	
Protein 1g	

Vitamin A 0%	•	Vitamin C 4%	
Calcium 0%	•	Iron 8%	

* Percent Daily Values are based on a 2,000 calorie diet. Your daily values may be higher or lower depending on your calorie needs.

7️⃣

	Calories	2,000	2,500
Total Fat	Less than	65g	80g
Sat Fat	Less than	20g	25g
Cholesterol	Less than	300mg	300mg
Sodium	Less than	2,400mg	2,400mg
Total Carbohydrate		300g	375g
Dietary Fiber		25g	30g

Calories per gram:

Fat 9   •   Carbohydrate 4   •   Protein 4

Understanding the Chart

To learn more about the chart, refer to the number labels on the chart and read the descriptions that follow.

1 title

The title gives a general idea about the chart's contents. This title says that the chart shows food labels.

2 subtitle

The subtitle explains what the chart is about in more detail than the title. This subtitle says the chart shows nutritional information on the label of a 10 oz. package of chocolate mint cookies.

3 heading

This food label heading gives the serving sizes. The new food labels feature more consistent serving sizes, showing both household and metric measures. This makes it easier to compare products.

4 Amount Per Serving

This category shows the calories per serving. It also shows the calories from fat. This information helps people meet dietary guidelines that recommend no more than 30 percent of calories from fat.

5 nutrients

Nutrients that are required on the label are those most important to consumers. Many people need to worry about getting too much of certain items like fat.

6 % Daily Value

The numbers under this column heading show how a food fits into the overall daily diet. You can use the values in this column to determine if a product is high or low in a nutrient. You can also use these values to compare the nutrients in different products.

7 reference values

Reference values help consumers adjust the daily values to meet their personal dietary needs. This chart helps you know the maximum amounts of fat, cholesterol, and sodium you should take in daily and the minimum amounts of carbohydrates and fiber you should eat each day.

The chart shows this information for someone who takes in approximately 2,000 calories a day (many older adults, children, and less active women) and someone who takes in 2,500 calories per day (active men, teenage boys, and very active women). For instance, it says that someone on a 2,000 calorie diet should take in *Less than* 65 grams of fat daily, while someone on a 2,500 calorie diet should take in *Less than* 80g.

 **Check Your Understanding 5.8.2**

Refer to this label to answer the questions that follow. Put a check (✓) next to the correct answers in the answer column.

Food Labeling

Nutritional information on the label of a 10 oz. package of chocolate mint cookies.

Nutrition Facts

Serving Size: 4 cookies (28g)
Servings Per Container: About 10

Amount Per Serving
Calories 150   Calories from Fat 70

	% Daily Value*
Total Fat 8g	12%
Saturated Fat 5g	25%
Cholesterol 0mg	0%
Sodium 70mg	3%
Total Carbohydrate 18g	6%
Dietary Fiber 0.5g	2%
Sugars 9g	
Protein 1g	

Vitamin A 0%	•	Vitamin C 4%
Calcium 0%	•	Iron 8%

* Percent Daily Values are based on a 2,000 calorie diet. Your daily values may be higher or lower depending on your calorie needs.

	Calories	2,000	2,500
Total Fat	Less than	65g	80g
Sat Fat	Less than	20g	25g
Cholesterol	Less than	300mg	300mg
Sodium	Less than	2,400mg	2,400mg
Total Carbohydrate		300g	375g
Dietary Fiber		25g	30g

Calories per gram:
Fat 9   •   Carbohydrate 4   •   Protein 4

Question	Answer
1. How many calories are in four chocolate mint cookies?	____ 28 calories ____ 150 calories ____ 70 calories
2. What percent of the daily value (intake) of saturated fat is in four cookies?	____ 12% ____ 25% ____ 6%
3. How many cookies would you have to eat to give you 100% of your daily amount of saturated fat?	____ 4 ____ 8 ____ 12 ____ 16
4. Homer wants to buy the cookies with the lower amount of sodium. He found some vanilla wafers that contain 100mg of sodium for a 28g serving. Should Homer buy the vanilla wafers or the chocolate mint cookies?	____ vanilla wafers ____ chocolate mint cookies
5. Brad wants to buy cookies that do not contain cholesterol. Do these cookies contain cholesterol?	____ Yes ____ No
6. Karen is a marathon runner. She needs more calories per day than most women to keep up her running. According the reference values at the bottom of the label, how many grams of carbohydrate should Karen take in each day?	____ 30g ____ 300g ____ 375g

5.9 Charts: Flexible Schedules, U.S. Retail Trade

5.9.1 U.S. Workers on Flexible Schedules

Workers on flexible schedules can vary the time they begin and end their work day. This chart compares the number of U.S. workers on flexible schedules in 1991 with the total number of workers. The chart also lets you see how the numbers of people on flexible schedules differs by age group.

① U.S. Workers on Flexible Schedules: 1991

② Age (years)	③ All Workers: Flexible and Set Schedules ⑤ (in thousands) ⑨	④ Workers With Flexible Schedules	
		⑥ Number (in thousands)	⑦ Percent
⑧ 16 - 19	1,413	⑩ 150	⑪ 10.6%
20 - 24	8,332	999	12.0%
25 - 34	25,523	4,008	15.7%
35 - 44	22,749	3,744	16.5%
45 - 54	14,306	2,184	15.3%
55 - 64	7,197	880	12.2%
65 +	933	153	16.4%

⑫ Source: U.S. Bureau of Labor Statistics

Understanding the Chart

To learn more about the chart above, refer to the number labels on the chart and read the descriptions below.

 title

The title gives a general idea about the chart's content. This title says the chart shows U.S. workers that are on flexible schedules in 1991.

 Age (years)

This heading identifies the category that shows the age groups of working people in the U.S. in 1991.

3▷ **All Workers (Flexible and Set Schedules)**

This heading identifies the category that shows the total number of working people in the U.S. in 1991.

4▷ **Workers With Flexible Schedules**

This heading identifies the category that shows the number and percent of working people in the U.S. who were on flexible schedules in 1991.

5▷ **(in thousands)**

This note tells you to multiply by 1,000 or add three zeros to each number that appears in this column. For example, the number 4,008 in this column represents 4,008,000 people.

6▷ **Number**

This heading identifies the category that shows the number of working people in the U.S. who were on flexible schedules in 1991.

7▷ **Percent**

This heading identifies the category that shows the percent of working people in the U.S. who were on flexible schedules in 1991.

8▷ **age**

The numbers in this column show the different age ranges for which data was collected.

9▷ **total number of workers**

The numbers in this column show the total number of workers of different ages that work on flexible and set schedules. The numbers are in thousands. For example, there are a total of 14,306,000 workers age 45-54.

10▷ **number of workers on flexible schedules**

The numbers in this column show the numbers of workers of different ages that work on a flexible schedule. The numbers are in thousands. For example, 3,744,000 of workers age 35-44 have flexible schedules.

11▷ **percent of workers on flexible schedules**

The numbers in this column show the percent of workers of different ages that work on a flexible schedule. For example, 15.7% of workers age 25-34 have flexible schedules.

Source: U.S. Bureau of Labor Statistics

This note tells you the source of the figures used in this chart.

 Check Your Understanding 5.9.1

Refer to this chart to answer the questions that follow. Put a check (✓) next to the correct answers in the answer column.

U.S. Workers on Flexible Schedules: 1991

Age (years)	All Workers: Flexible and Set Schedules (in thousands)	Workers With Flexible Schedules	
		Number (in thousands)	Percent
16 - 19	1,413	150	10.6%
20 - 24	8,332	999	12.0%
25 - 34	25,523	4,008	15.7%
35 - 44	22,749	3,744	16.5%
45 - 54	14,306	2,184	15.3%
55 - 64	7,197	880	12.2%
65 +	933	153	16.4%

Source: U.S. Bureau of Labor Statistics

Question	Answer
1. How many U.S. workers age 55-64 had flexible schedules in 1991?	___ 7,197 ___ 880 ___ 880,000
2. Which age group had 16.5% of its workers on a flexible schedule in 1991?	___ 65+ ___ 45-54 ___ 35-44
3. Which age group had the greatest number of workers on flexible schedules in 1991?	___ 25-34 ___ 35-44 ___ 45-54
4. Which age group had the smallest percent of its workers on flexible schedules?	___ 16-19 ___ 20-24 ___ 55-64
5. In 1991, how many more flexible schedule workers were in the 35-44 age group than in the 65+ age group?	___ 3,591 ___ 3,591,000 ___ 1%
6. Cheryl wants to start a newsletter called *Flextime* for workers on flexible schedules. Which two age groups would have made up her largest audiences in 1991?	___ 16-19, 25-38 ___ 25-34, 35-44 ___ 35-44, 65+

5.9.2 Retail Businesses, Employees, and Payroll

This chart will help you learn more about which types of businesses are growing the fastest by looking at changes between 1989 and 1992. You will be able to compare the changes in number of businesses, the number of employees in each kind of business, and how much those businesses pay their employees.

①U.S. Retail Trade — Businesses, Employees, and Payroll: 1989 and 1990

②A comparison of the number of retail businesses, the number of people employed in those businesses, and the total amount paid to retail employees in 1989 and 1990.

③ Kind of Business	④ Businesses (1,000)		⑤ Employees (1,000)		⑥ Payroll (bil. dol.)	
	⑦ 1989	⑧ 1990	⑨ 1989	⑩ 1990	⑪ 1989	⑫ 1990
Building materials and garden supplies	71.2	71.9	698	703	11.4	11.9
General merchandise stores	35.8	36.6	2,082	2,135	21.9	22.9
Food stores	183.9	186.1	3,012	3,124	33.6	35.8
Car dealers and service stations	208.2	207.3	2,129	2,104	39.4	40.0
Clothing and accessory stores	147.5	150.2	1,168	1,193	11.5	12.2
Furniture and home furnishings stores	104.6	108.1	734	749	11.8	12.3
Eating and drinking places	391.5	402.6	6,288	6,461	46.1	49.6
Miscellaneous retail	334.7	349.0	2,386	2,487	30.7	33.2

⑬ Source: U.S. Bureau of the Census

Understanding the Chart

To learn more about the chart above, refer to the number labels on the chart and read the descriptions below.

 title

> The title gives a general idea about the chart's content. This title says the chart shows businesses, employees, and payroll in the U.S. retail trade in 1989 and 1990.

▷2 **subtitle**

The subtitle explains what the chart is about in more detail than the title. This subtitle says the chart shows a comparison of the number of retail businesses, the number of people employed in those businesses, and the total amount paid to retail employees in 1989 and 1990.

▷3 **Kind of Business**

This column heading has the different types of retail businesses listed under it.

▷4 **Businesses (1,000)**

This heading tells you all numbers under this column show the number of U.S. retail businesses in 1989 and 1990. These numbers are in thousands. So you will need to multiply each number by 1,000 to get the actual numbers. For example, the number 71.2 on the chart represents 71,200 businesses.

▷5 **Employees (1,000)**

This heading tells you that all numbers under this column show the number of employees in U.S. retail businesses in 1989 and 1990. These numbers are in thousands. For example, the number 2,082 on the chart represents 2,082,000 people.

▷6 **Payroll (bil. dol.)**

This heading shows that all numbers under this column represent the amount of money paid to employees in U.S. retail businesses in 1989 and 1990. These numbers are in billions of dollars. For example, the number 11.4 on the chart represents $11,400,000,000, or $11.4 billion.

▷7 **Establishments, 1989**

The numbers in this column show how many thousands of different retail businesses there were in 1989. For example, in 1989 there were 183,900 food stores.

▷8 **Establishments, 1990**

The numbers in this column show how many thousands of different retail businesses there were in 1990. For example, in 1990 there were 186,100 food stores.

Employees, 1989

The numbers in this column show how many thousands of employees were in different retail businesses in 1989. For example, in 1989 there were 6,288,000 employees working in eating and drinking places.

 Employees, 1990

The numbers in this column show how many thousands of employees were in different retail businesses in 1990. For example, in 1990 there were 749,000 employees working in furniture and home furnishings stores.

Payroll, 1989

The numbers in this column show the amount of money paid to employees in different U.S. retail businesses in 1989. For example, $11,500,000,000 ($11.5 billion) was paid to employees working in clothing and accessory stores in 1989.

Payroll, 1990

The numbers in this column show the amount of money paid to employees in different U.S. retail businesses in 1990. For example, $22,900,000,000 ($22.9 billion) was paid to employees working in general merchandise stores in 1990.

 Source: U.S. Bureau of the Census

This note tells you the source of the figures used in this chart.

 **Check Your Understanding 5.9.2**

Refer to this chart to answer the questions that follow. Put a check (✓) next to the correct answers in the answer column.

U.S. Retail Trade — Businesses, Employees, and Payroll: 1989 and 1990

A comparison of the number of retail businesses, the number of people employed in those businesses, and the total amount paid to retail employees in 1989 and 1990.

Kind of Business	Businesses (1,000)		Employees (1,000)		Payroll (bil. dol.)	
	1989	1990	1989	1990	1989	1990
Building materials and garden supplies	71.2	71.9	698	703	11.4	11.9
General merchandise stores	35.8	36.6	2,082	2,135	21.9	22.9
Food stores	183.9	186.1	3,012	3,124	33.6	35.8
Car dealers and service stations	208.2	207.3	2,129	2,104	39.4	40.0
Clothing and accessory stores	147.5	150.2	1,168	1,193	11.5	12.2
Furniture and home furnishings stores	104.6	108.1	734	749	11.8	12.3
Eating and drinking places	391.5	402.6	6,288	6,461	46.1	49.6
Miscellaneous retail	334.7	349.0	2,386	2,487	30.7	33.2

Source: U.S. Bureau of the Census

Question	Answer
1. How many people worked for car dealers and service stations in 1990?	___ 2,129,000 ___ 2,104 ___ 2,104,000
2. What kind of business had a payroll of $11.8 billion in 1989?	___ Furniture and home furnishings stores ___ Clothing and accessory stores ___ Building materials and garden supplies

3. How many furniture and home furnishing stores were there in 1990?	___ 108,100 ___ 104,600 ___ 749,000
4. In which kind of business did the number of employees decrease between 1989 and 1990?	___ Food stores ___ General merchandise stores ___ Car dealers and service stations
5. Which kind of business had the fewest stores in 1990?	___ Food stores ___ Building materials and garden supplies ___ General merchandise stores
6. Susan is writing a report for her careers class. In her report, she wants to use data to suggest which retail industry had the largest payroll increase between 1989 and 1990. Which retail industry increased its payroll the most during this period?	___ General merchandise stores ___ Apparel and accessory stores ___ Eating and drinking places

5.10 Line Graphs: Bicycle Trade, School Enrollment

5.10.1 U.S. Bicycle Trade

Line graphs compare different pieces of information. This line graph shows the number of bikes sold in the U.S. by American companies and foreign companies between 1970 and 1991. One line shows the number of bikes sold in the U.S. by American companies, and the other line shows the number sold by foreign companies. The lines rise and fall on the graph, depending on whether bike sales increased or decreased.

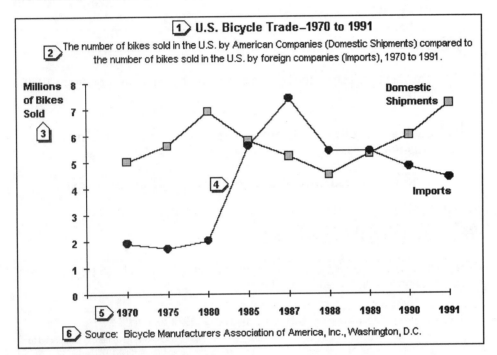

Understanding the Graph

To learn more about the graph above, refer to the number labels on the graph and read the following descriptions.

 title

> The title gives general information about the line graph's contents. This title explains that the graph shows bicycle trading activity in the U.S. between 1970 and 1991.

subtitle

> The subtitle describes the line graph in more detail than the title. This subtitle says that the line graph compares the number of bikes sold in the U.S. by American companies (Domestic Shipments) to the number sold by foreign companies (Imports) between 1970 and 1991.

Millions of bikes sold

The numbers running down the side of the graph show how many millions of bikes were sold.

 line on the chart

This is a line on the chart. Lines on the chart represent bike sales. One line (▣—▣) shows the number of bikes sold in the U.S. by American companies, and the other line (●—●) shows the number sold by foreign companies. Lines that rise show an increase in sales; lines that fall show a decrease in sales.

⑤ **year**

The numbers across the bottom of the graph represent years from 1970 to 1991.

⑥ **Source: Bicycle Manufacturers Association of America, Inc., Washington D.C.**

This note tells you where the figures used in this chart came from.

 Check Your Understanding 5.10.1

Refer to this graph to answer the questions that follow. Put a check (✓) next to the correct answers in the answer column.

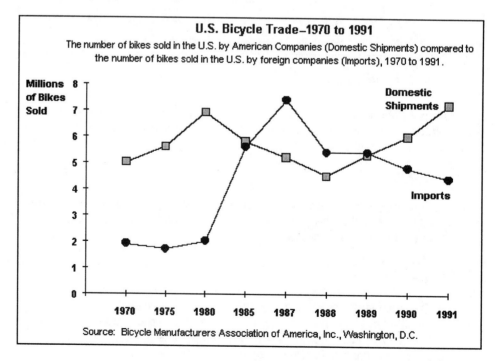

U.S. Bicycle Trade–1970 to 1991

The number of bikes sold in the U.S. by American Companies (Domestic Shipments) compared to the number of bikes sold in the U.S. by foreign companies (Imports), 1970 to 1991.

Source: Bicycle Manufacturers Association of America, Inc., Washington, D.C.

Question	Answer
1. In 1991, more bikes were sold by	___ U.S. companies ___ foreign companies
2. In 1990, how many bikes were sold by U.S. companies?	___ approximately 5 million ___ approximately 5.5 million ___ approximately 6 million
3. Which year did foreign bikes have their highest amount of sales?	___ 1980 ___ 1987 ___ 1991
4. When did the number of bikes sold by U.S. companies reach its lowest amount of sales?	___ just before foreign bike sales reached its highest point ___ the same year foreign bike sales reached their highest point ___ the year after foreign bike sales reached their highest point
5. By 1991, how many more bikes were sold by U.S. companies than by foreign companies?	___ about 1 million ___ about 2 million ___ about 3 million
6. Morris writes articles for sports and outdoor magazines. He's preparing an article on trends in cycling. He wants to know when foreign bicycles first became popular. Between which years did foreign bicycle sales increase the most?	___ between 1970-75 ___ between 1980-85 ___ between 1990-91

5.10.2 U.S. School Enrollment

Line graphs compare different pieces of information. This line graph shows the number of students enrolled in U.S. schools between 1970 and 2000. The shaded area of the graph includes the estimated enrollment between 1990 and 2000. The lines rise and fall on the graph, depending on whether school enrollment increased or decreased.

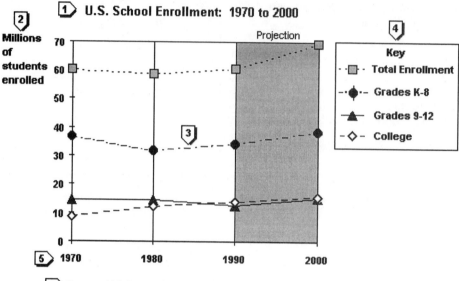

Understanding the Graph

To learn more about the graph, refer to the number labels on the graph and read the descriptions below.

1 **title**

The title gives general information about the line graph's contents. This title explains that the graph shows school enrollment in the U.S. between 1970 and 2000.

2 **Millions of students enrolled**

This heading shows that the numbers running down the side of the graph show how many millions of students were enrolled in school.

3 **line on the chart**

This is a line on the chart. Lines on the chart represent different groups of students that are enrolled in school. Lines that rise show an increase in school enrollment; lines that fall show a decrease in school enrollment.

4 **key**

The key gives information about the chart. Each type of line represents a different group of students on the graph.

5 **year**

The numbers across the bottom of the graph represent years from 1970 to 2000.

6 **Source: U.S. Department of Education**

This note tells you where the figures used in this chart came from.

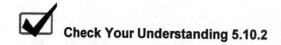

Check Your Understanding 5.10.2

Refer to this graph to answer the questions that follow. Put a check (✓) next to the correct answers in the answer column.

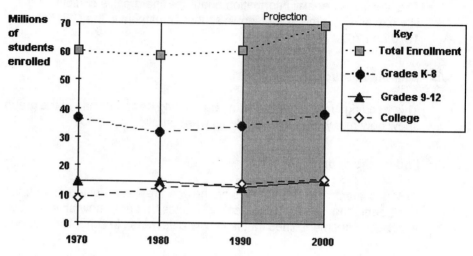

Source: U.S. Department of Education

Question	Answer
1. Which grade levels consistently had the most students enrolled during 1970 to 1990?	___ Grades K-8 ___ Grades 9-12 ___ College
2. Between 1970 and 1980, which grade levels had an increase in the number of students enrolled?	___ Grades K-8 ___ Grades 9-12 ___ College
3. Between 1970 and 1980, which grade levels had a decrease in the number of students enrolled?	___ Grades K-8 ___ Grades 9-12 ___ College
4. The number of students enrolled on which two levels will be about the same by the year 2000?	___ Grades K-8, Grades K-12 ___ Grades 9-12, College ___ Grades K-8, College
5. In the year 2000, approximately how many more students will be enrolled in Grades K-8 than in Grades 9-12?	___ about 15 million more ___ about 25 million more ___ about 35 million more
6. A committee is preparing a bulletin for the National School Board Association. The committee wants to know approximately how many more students will be enrolled in school at all levels by the year 2000, compared to 1990.	___ 2 million more ___ 5 million more ___ 10 million more

5.11 Maps: Street, Park

5.11.1 Richmore City Center

Maps represent and give information about places. This street map shows the location of streets, public buildings and a park in Richmore city center.

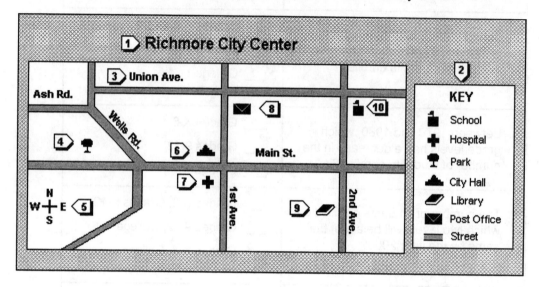

Understanding the Map

To learn more about the map above, refer to the number labels on the map and read the descriptions below.

 title

    The title gives you a general idea of what the map is about. This title tells you that the map will show the city center of Richmore.

2⟩ key

The key tells you what the symbols on the map represent. For example, a picture of a tree stands for a park. The symbols are put into the map to show the location of the buildings or places they represent.

3⟩ Union Ave.

This is the name of a street in the city center of Richmore. The streets are shown with lines. All streets have a name label.

4⟩ park (🌳)

By looking in the key, you can tell that this symbol stands for a park.

5⟩ compass

This compass shows direction. The letters *N, S, E,* and *W* stand for *north, south, east,* and *west.*

6⟩ symbol for city hall (⛪)

Check in the key and you will see that this symbol stands for the city hall building.

7⟩ symbol for Hospital (✚)

By looking in the key, you can tell that this symbol stands for a hospital.

8⟩ symbol for post office (✉)

This symbol stands for a post office.

9⟩ symbol for library (📖)

This symbol stands for a library.

10⟩ symbol for school (🏫)

By looking in the key, you can tell that this symbol stands for a school.

 **Check Your Understanding 5.11.1**

Refer to this map to answer the questions that follow. Put a check (✓) next to the correct answers in the answer column.

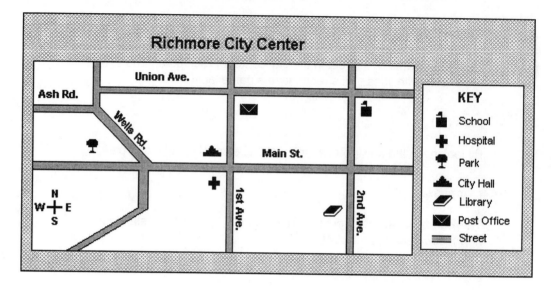

Question	Answer
1. On which street is the library located?	___ 1st Ave. ___ 2nd Ave. ___ Main St.
2. Which building is immediately north of the hospital?	___ school ___ city hall ___ library
3. To get from the school to the hospital, you would go down	___ Union Ave. and 1st Ave. ___ Union Ave. and Wells St. ___ 2nd Ave. and Ash Rd.
4. About how far is the post office from the city hall?	___ one block ___ two blocks ___ three blocks
5. The ambulance needs to get from the hospital to the city park as quickly as possible. Which direction should it travel to get there?	___ north ___ south ___ east ___ west
6. The Richmore city council wants to build a new city park three blocks east of the current park. This new city park will be located closest to which building?	___ School ___ Hospital ___ Post Office

5.11.2 Lake Wanosh Recreation Area

Maps represent and give information about places. This map shows recreation facilities at Lake Wanosh Recreation Area.

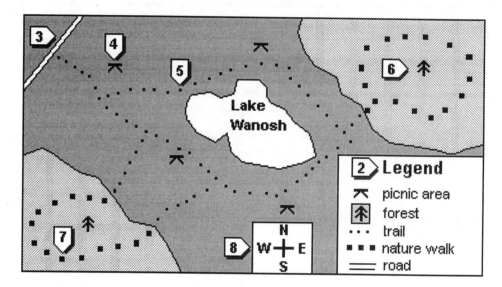

Understanding the Map

To learn more about the map, refer to the number labels on the map and read the descriptions below.

1 title

The title gives you a general idea of what the map is about. This title tells you that the map will show Lake Wanosh recreation area.

2 key

The key tells you what the symbols on the map represent. For example, a picture of a tree stands for a forest.

3 symbol for road (═)

By looking at the key, you can tell that this symbol stands for a road.

4 symbol for picnic table (⋔)

Check the key and you will see that this symbol stands for a picnic area.

5 symbol for trail (···)

This symbol shows a trail on the map.

6 symbol for forest (🌲)

Check in the key and you will see that this symbol stands for a forest.

7 symbol for nature walk (▪ ▪)

By looking in the key, you can tell that this symbol stands for a nature walk.

8 compass

The compass shows direction. The letters *N, S, E,* and *W* stand for *north, south, east,* and *west.*

Check Your Understanding 5.11.2

Refer to this map to answer the questions that follow. Put a check (✓) next to the correct answers in the answer column.

Lake Wanosh Recreation Area

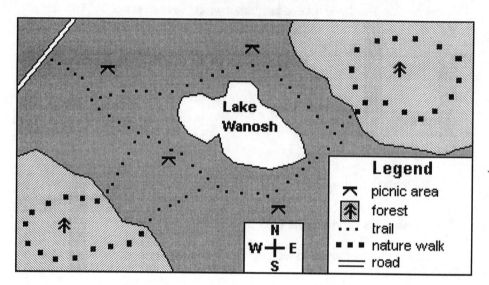

Question	Answer
1. On which side of the lake is the road located?	___ east side ___ west side
2. How many picnic areas are on the map?	___ 3 ___ 4 ___ 5
3. What does the smallest dotted line on the map represent?	___ trail ___ nature walk ___ road
4. In which directions are the nature walks located from the lake?	___ northwest and northeast ___ southwest and northeast ___ southeast and northwest
5. Finish this statement: There are no picnic areas ___ of the lake.	___ north ___ south ___ east ___ west
6. Assume that all of the trails on the map are drawn to the same distance scale. It takes about an hour and 15 minutes to take the trail around the lake. Would Roger have time to take the lake trail and do both nature walks in an hour and a half?	___ Yes ___ Probably not

5.12 Maps: State, U.S.

5.12.1 Mileages — Colorado

Maps represent and give information about places. This map shows the mileages between some towns and cities in Colorado.

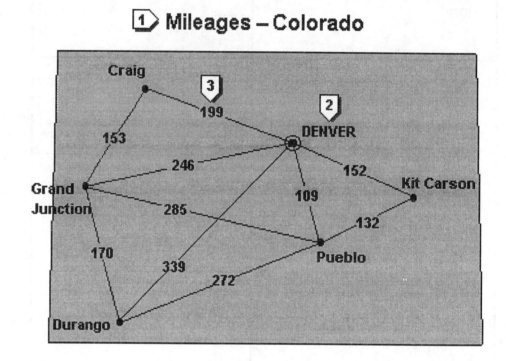

① Mileages – Colorado

Understanding the Map

To learn more about the map, refer to the number labels on the map and read the descriptions below.

1 **title**

The title gives you a general idea of what the map is about. This title tells you that the map shows mileages in Colorado.

2 **names of towns**

The names of some of the towns and cities in Colorado are on this map. Each dot stands for a town or city. DENVER is in capital letters because Denver is the capital of Colorado.

3 **mileages**

Each number shows the miles between the two dots (towns) connected by the line.

Check Your Understanding 5.12.1

Refer to this map to answer the questions that follow. Put a check (✓) next to the correct answers in the answer column.

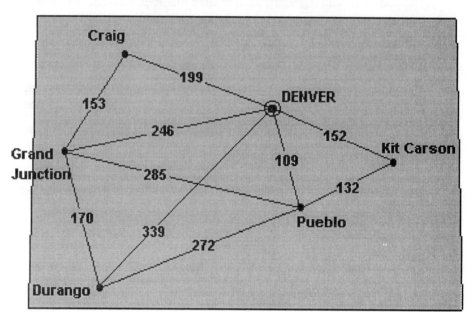

Mileages – Colorado

Question	Answer
1. How far is Durango from Denver?	___ 339 miles ___ 285 miles ___ 272 miles
2. Which of these places is closest to Grand Junction?	___ Pueblo ___ Kit Carson ___ Denver
3. Craig is closest to which other town?	___ Denver ___ Grand Junction ___ Durango
4. Which place is furthest from the capital, Denver?	___ Durango ___ Craig ___ Grand Junction
5. Derek wants to ride his bike from Durango to Grand Junction and back. How far will he be riding?	___ about 153 miles ___ about 170 miles ___ about 340 miles
6. The Gomez family wants to take a vacation from Denver to Pueblo and stop some other places along the way. Which trip would be shorter?	___ Denver, Grand Junction, Pueblo, Denver ___ Denver, Pueblo, Durango, Denver

5.12.2 U.S. Population

Maps represent and give information about places. This map shows population information about each state.

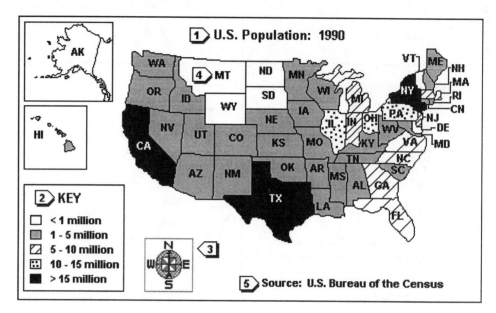

Understanding the Map

To learn more about the map, refer to the number labels on the map and read the descriptions below.

1 title

This title tells you that the map shows the population in the U.S. in 1990.

2 key

The key tells you what the different shaded areas on the map represent. The numbers represent people. The < sign means less than, and the > sign means greater than.

3 compass

This compass shows direction. The letters *N, S, E,* and *W* stand for *north, south, east,* and *west.*

4 state names

The letters on the map are abbreviations for state names.

5 **Source: U.S. Bureau of the Census**
This is the source of the information shown in the chart. The figures used in the chart come from the U.S. Bureau of the Census.

Check Your Understanding 5.12.2

Refer to this map to answer the questions that follow. Put a check (✓) next to the correct answers in the answer column.

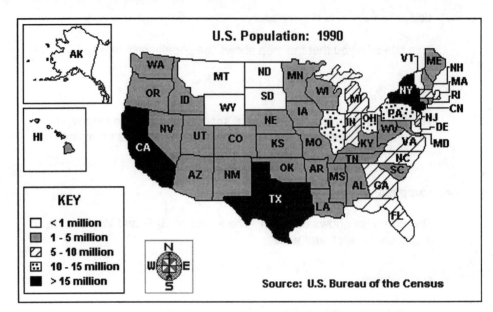

Question	Answer
1. What was the population of Illinois (IL) in 1990?	___ < 1 million ___ 1-5 million ___ 5-10 million ___ 10-15 million
2. Which states had a population of 5-10 million in 1990? (Mark all that apply.)	___ North Carolina (NC) ___ California (CA) ___ Ohio (OH) ___ Michigan (MI)
3. How many states had populations of less than one million in 1990?	___ 3 ___ 4 ___ 5 ___ 6
4. Finish this statement: All the states with populations of 5-10 million in 1990 were found in the ___ half of the United States.	___ western ___ eastern
5. The number of representatives each state can have in the U.S. House of Representatives depends on the population of the state. The greater the population, the more representatives a state has. Which of these states has the most representatives in Congress?	___ Kansas (KS) ___ North Carolina (NC) ___ Hawaii (HI) ___ Pennsylvania (PA)
6. An educational textbook publisher wants to make sure its textbooks meet the requirements set by the most populous states. Which states' requirements should they check first?	___ Virginia (VA), North Carolina (NC), Florida (FL) ___ Illinois (IL), Ohio (OH), Pennsylvania (PA) ___ New York (NY), California (CA), Texas (TX)

5.13 Maps: Layout, Floor Plan

5.13.1 North Campus — Dennington College

This map shows the layout of a college campus. It gives information about the walkways and the locations of the different buildings.

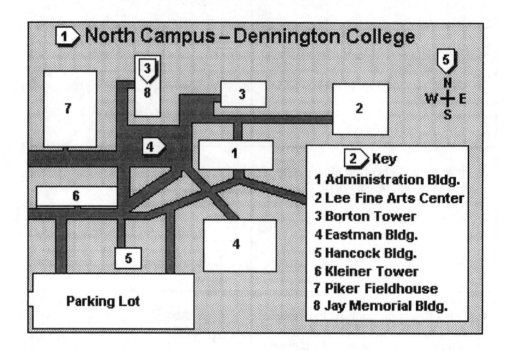

Understanding the Map

To learn more about the map, refer to the number labels on the map and read the descriptions below.

1⟩ title

The title gives you a general idea of what the map is about. This title tells you that the map shows the North Campus of Dennington College.

2⟩ key

The key tells you what the numbers on the map represent. For example, building number 7 is the Piker Fieldhouse.

3⟩ building

The rectangular white boxes on the map represent buildings.

4⟩ sidewalk

The shaded areas represent sidewalks.

5⟩ compass

This compass shows direction. The letters *N, S, E,* and *W* stand for *north, south, east,* and *west.*

Check Your Understanding 5.13.1

Refer to this map to answer the questions that follow. Put a check (✓) next to the correct answers in the answer column.

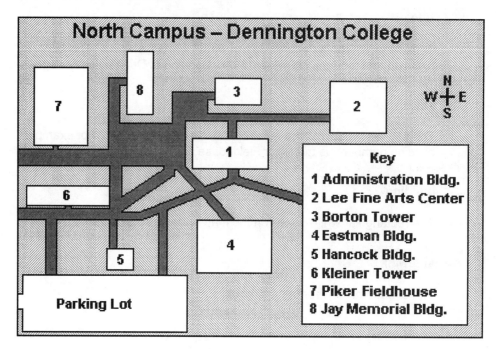

Question	Answer
1. Which building is nearest to the parking lot?	___ Hancock Building ___ Kleiner Tower ___ Piker Fieldhouse
2. Which is the nearest building east of Piker Fieldhouse?	___ Jay Memorial Building ___ Kleiner Tower ___ Borton Tower
3. Which building is the greatest walking distance from the Lee Fine Arts Center?	___ Administration Building ___ Jay Memorial Building ___ Hancock Building
4. The college president's office is on the south side of the Administration Building. If she looks out of her office window, what building does she see?	___ Borton Tower ___ Eastman Building ___ Lee Fine Arts Center
5. Assume that all walkways on the map are drawn to the same distance scale. It takes Lorraine 10 minutes to walk from the Hancock Building to the Jay Memorial Building. She plans to take a class in the Lee Fine Arts Center that ends at 9:00 a.m. Can she expect to be on time to her next class that starts at 9:10 a.m. in the Borton Tower?	___ Yes ___ No
6. Assume that all walkways on the map are drawn to the same distance scale. Edward has his first class of the afternoon in the Kleiner Tower and his next class in the Eastman Building. His friend, Nichole, has a class in the Lee Fine Arts center and her next class in the Borton Tower. Who has to walk further between classes?	___ Edward ___ Nichole

5.13.2 Clifton Library Floor Plan

Maps provide information about places. This map shows the floor plan of a library. It gives useful information about the locations of different types of reference sources.

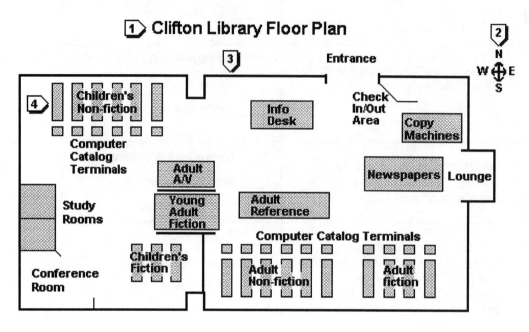

Understanding the Map

To learn more about the map, refer to the number labels on the map and read the descriptions below.

1 **title**

The title gives you a general idea of what the map is about. This title tells you that the map shows the floor plan of Clifton Library.

2 **compass**

This compass shows direction. The letters *N, S, E, and W* stand for *north, south, east*, and *west.*

3 **walls of the building**

The dark lines show the walls of the library.

4 **bookcases**

The long, thin, rectangles are bookcases.

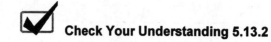 **Check Your Understanding 5.13.2**

Refer to this map to answer the questions that follow. Put a check (✓) next to the correct answers in the answer column.

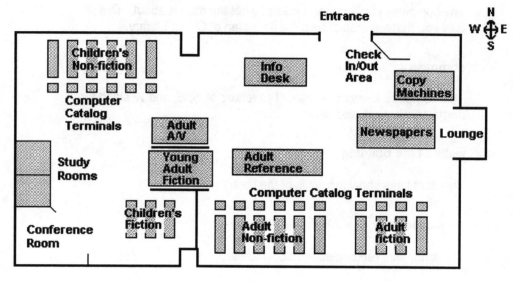

Clifton Library Floor Plan

Question	Answer
1. What is west of the Young Adult Fiction section?	___ Adult Reference ___ Study Rooms ___ Children's Fiction
2. Where are the Adult Non-Fiction books found?	___ south of the information desk ___ west of the information desk ___ east of the information desk
3. Are there any restrooms on this floor of the library?	___ Yes ___ No
4. You are in the Adult Reference section and decide you want to use a copy machine. Which section do you have to walk past to get to the copy machines?	___ Adult fiction ___ Children's fiction ___ Newspapers
5. Amber wants to let her kids look for books in the Children's Fiction section while she is studying. She wants to study near her children to make sure they keep quiet. Where should she sit?	___ near the Study Rooms ___ next to the Adult Reference section ___ in the Lounge
6. Barry wants to check out a video on how to plant a garden. Where should he go to find the video?	___ the Adult Reference section ___ the Adult Non-fiction section ___ the Adult Audio/Visual (A/V) section

5.14 Pie Charts: U.S. Waste, Coastal Populations

5.14.1 U.S. Waste Management

Pie charts show how parts of a whole relate to each other. This pie chart shows how U.S. communities disposed of their waste in 1990.

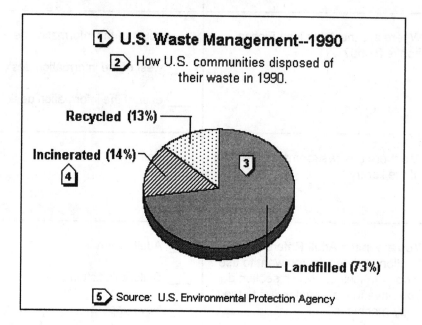

1 **U.S. Waste Management--1990**

2 How U.S. communities disposed of their waste in 1990.

Recycled (13%)

Incinerated (14%)

3

Landfilled (73%)

5 Source: U.S. Environmental Protection Agency

Understanding the Pie Chart

To learn more about the pie chart, refer to the number labels on the pie chart and read the descriptions below.

1 **title**

The title explains what the chart is about generally. For example, this title says that the chart will show how waste is managed in the U.S.

2 **subtitle**

A subtitle explains in greater detail what the chart is about. For example, this subtitle says the chart will show how U.S. communities disposed of their waste in 1990. The chart will show this information in percent.

3 **piece of the pie**

Each piece of the pie shows one category of waste disposal. The size of the piece shows the proportion of waste disposed by each method. For example, the piece that represents Recycled is about the same size as the piece that represents Incinerated, because 13% is almost the same as 14%.

4 **label**

Each label names a piece of the pie. While the size of the piece shows approximately how much U.S. communities use this method of waste disposal, the number in the label gives an exact amount. For example, this chart tells you that 73% of the waste in the U.S. was disposed of by sending it to a landfill.

5 **Source: U.S. Environmental Protection Agency**

This is the source of the information shown in the chart.

Check Your Understanding 5.14.1

Refer to this pie chart to answer the questions that follow. Put a check (✓) next to the correct answers in the answer column.

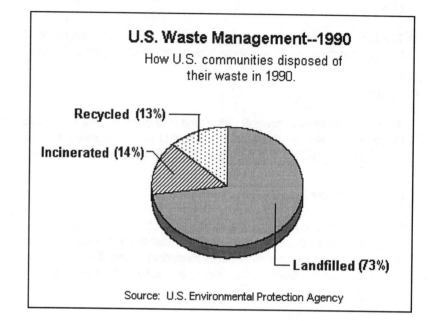

U.S. Waste Management--1990
How U.S. communities disposed of their waste in 1990.

Recycled (13%)

Incinerated (14%)

Landfilled (73%)

Source: U.S. Environmental Protection Agency

Question	Answer
1. According to this chart, what proportion of the waste in the U.S. was recycled in 1990?	___ 13% ___ 14% ___ 73%
2. What was the second most popular method of waste management in 1990?	___ Landfill ___ Recycling ___ Incineration

3. What assumptions MUST you make when interpreting this chart? (Mark all that apply.)	____ the whole pie represents all waste disposed of in the U.S. ____ each piece of the pie shows one method of disposing of waste ____ all the percents listed add up to 100%
4. Finish this statement: If one of the methods of disposal increased, one or both of the other pieces of the pie would have to ____.	____ get smaller ____ stay the same ____ get bigger
5. Finish this statement: About ____ of all the waste disposed of in the U.S. is sent to landfills.	____ 1/4 ____ 1/2 ____ 3/4
6. Environmental groups want to determine if their efforts to get communities to do more recycling is having any effect. You could say "yes" if you compared pie charts similar to this one for future years and found that the recycling piece _____.	____ got smaller ____ stayed the same ____ got bigger

5.14.2 U.S. Coastal Population

Pie charts show how parts of a whole relate to each other. This pie chart shows where the coastal population of the U.S. lives.

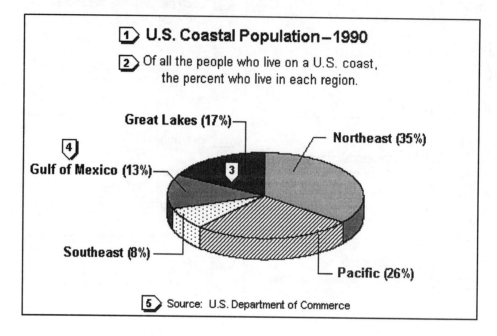

Understanding the Pie Chart

To learn more about the pie chart, refer to the number labels on the pie chart and read the descriptions below.

1 **title**

The title explains what the chart is about generally. For example, this title says that the chart will show where the U.S coastal population lives.

2 **subtitle**

A subtitle explains in greater detail what the chart is about. For example, this subtitle says the chart will show the percent of U.S. coastal dwellers who live in each region.

3 **piece of the pie**

Each piece of the pie shows one coastal region. The size of the piece shows the proportion of U.S. coastal dwellers in that region. For example, the piece that represents the Northeast is about the same size as the combined pieces that represent the Pacific and Southeast, because 35% is almost the same as 26% plus 8%, which equals 34%.

4 **label**

Each label names a piece of the pie. While the size of the piece shows approximately the proportion of U.S. coastal dwellers in that region, the number in the label gives an exact amount. For example, this chart tells you that 13% of the U.S. coastal population lives along the coast of the Gulf of Mexico.

5 **Source: U.S. Department of Commerce**

This is the source of the information shown in the chart.

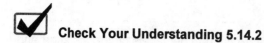 **Check Your Understanding 5.14.2**

Refer to this pie chart to answer the questions that follow. Put a check (✓) next to the correct answers in the answer column.

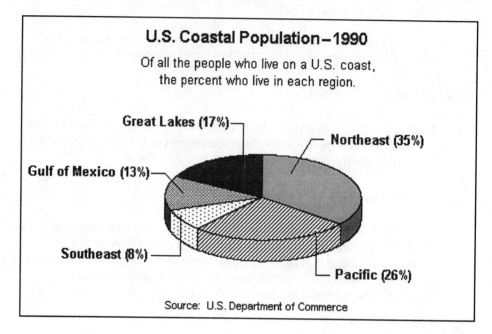

U.S. Coastal Population – 1990

Of all the people who live on a U.S. coast, the percent who live in each region.

Great Lakes (17%)

Northeast (35%)

Gulf of Mexico (13%)

Southeast (8%)

Pacific (26%)

Source: U.S. Department of Commerce

Question	Answer
1. According to this chart, what proportion of U.S. coastal dwellers lived on the Great Lakes shoreline in 1990?	___ 35% ___ 13% ___ 17%
2. Which region had the smallest percentage of coastal dwellers?	___ Southeast ___ Gulf of Mexico ___ Great Lakes
3. Finish this statement: About ___ of the U.S. coastal population lives along the Pacific Coast.	___ 1/4 ___ 1/3 ___ 1/2
4. Which two areas together have about the same number of coastal dwellers as the Great Lakes region?	___ Pacific and Southeast ___ Gulf of Mexico and Southeast ___ Gulf of Mexico and Pacific
5. The Great Lakes region had what percent fewer coastal dwellers than the Pacific region in 1990?	___ 4% ___ 9% ___ 18%
6. The U.S. Coast Guard wants to send special safety brochures to all coastal dwellers. Which region of the country should it target first in order to reach the most coastal dwellers?	___ Pacific ___ Great Lakes ___ Northeast

5.15 Pie Charts: Recording Media, Meat Consumed

5.15.1 U.S. Manufacturer's Shipments of Recording Media

Pie charts show how parts of a whole relate to each other. Sometimes it is useful to use two pie charts to compare how the parts of two wholes differ. This example shows charts representing information for different years.

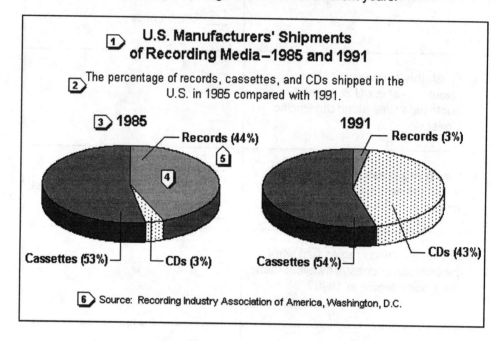

1 > U.S. Manufacturers' Shipments of Recording Media – 1985 and 1991

2 > The percentage of records, cassettes, and CDs shipped in the U.S. in 1985 compared with 1991.

3 > 1985
Records (44%) **5**
4
Cassettes (53%) — CDs (3%)

1991
Records (3%)
Cassettes (54%) — CDs (43%)

6 > Source: Recording Industry Association of America, Washington, D.C.

Understanding the Pie Chart

To learn more about the pie chart, refer to the number labels on the pie chart and read the descriptions below.

1 ▷ title

The title explains what the charts are about generally. For example, this title says that the pie charts will compare shipments of different types of recording media in 1985 to shipments in 1991.

2 ▷ subtitle

A subtitle explains in greater detail what the charts are about. For example, this subtitle says the charts will show the percentage of records, cassettes, and CDs shipped in the U.S. in 1985 compared with 1991.

3 ▷ year

The numbers at the top of each pie chart represent the years 1985 and 1991.

4 ▷ piece of the pie

Each piece of the pie shows one type of recording media. The size of the piece shows the proportion of that type of recording media compared to the other types. For example, the piece that represents CDs on the 1985 chart is the same size as the piece that represents records on the 1991 chart; both are 3%.

5 ▷ label

Each label names a piece of the pie. While the size of the piece shows approximately the proportion of that type of recording media, the number in the label gives an exact amount. For example, the chart for 1985 tells you that 44% of U.S. shipments of recording media were records.

6 ▷ Source: Recording Industry Association of America, Washington, D. C.

This is the source of the information shown in the chart.

 **Check Your Understanding 5.15.1**

Refer to these pie charts to answer the questions that follow. Put a check (✓) next to the correct answers in the answer column.

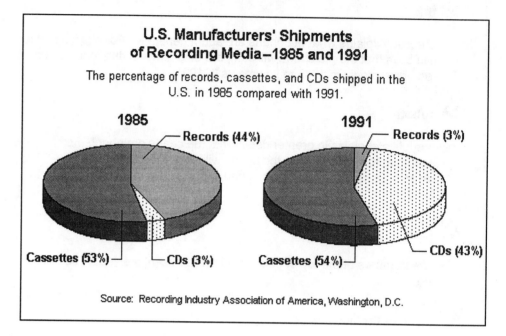

Question	Answer
1. In 1985, which type of media had the second largest percentage of total shipments?	___ CDs ___ Cassettes ___ Records
2. In 1991, which type of recording media had the second largest percentage of total shipments?	___ Records ___ Cassettes ___ CDs
3. In 1991, what was the percentage of records shipped?	___ 3% ___ 54% ___ 43%
4. Finish this statement: Cassettes made up a little over ___ the recording media being shipped in 1991.	___ 1/3 ___ 1/2 ___ 2/3
5. Jared runs a music store. If he assumes 1991 shipments reflect consumer demand, what percentage of his inventory should he expect to have in CDs?	___ 5-10% ___ 20-30% ___ 40-50%
6. A media magazine predicts that sales of CD players will continue to increase. More and more people will turn to CD players to replace their aging cassette players. Based on this information, how do you think the CD piece of the pie will compare to the cassette piece in a few years?	___ the CD piece will stay about the same sizes in the 1991 pie ___ the CD piece will get bigger than the cassette piece ___ the CD piece will be the same size as the cassette piece

5.15.2 Changes in U.S. Meat Consumption Per Person

The following two pie charts are useful to compare how the consumption of different types of meat changed during different years.

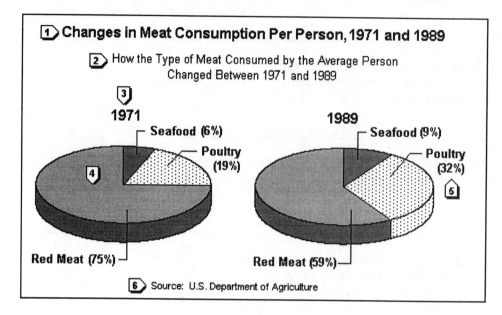

Understanding the Pie Chart

To learn more about the pie chart, refer to the number labels on the pie chart and read the descriptions below.

1 **title**

The title explains what the charts are about generally. For example, this title says that the pie charts will compare changes in U.S. meat consumption per person between 1971 and 1989.

2 **subtitle**

A subtitle explains in greater detail what the charts are about. For example, this subtitle says the charts will show how the type of meat consumed by the average person changed between 1971 and 1989. This information is shown in percentages.

3 **year**

The numbers at the top of each pie chart represent the years 1971 and 1989.

4 **piece of the pie**

Each piece of the pie shows one type of meat. The size of the piece shows the proportion of that type of meat compared to the other types. For example, on the 1971 chart, the piece that represents Red Meat is three times the size of the Poultry and Seafood categories combined.

5 **label**

Each label names a piece of the pie. While the size of the piece shows approximately the proportion of that type of meat, the number in the label gives an exact amount. For example, the chart for 1989 tells you that during that year 32% of meat eaten by the average person in the U.S. was poultry.

6 **Source: U.S. Department of Agriculture**

This is the source of the information shown in the chart.

 **Check Your Understanding 5.15.2**

Refer to these pie charts to answer the questions that follow. Put a check (✓) next to the correct answers in the answer column.

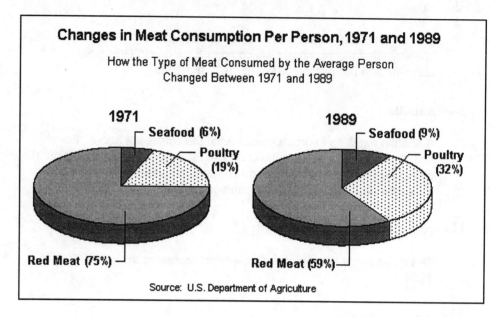

Changes in Meat Consumption Per Person, 1971 and 1989

How the Type of Meat Consumed by the Average Person
Changed Between 1971 and 1989

1971
Seafood (6%)
Poultry (19%)
Red Meat (75%)

1989
Seafood (9%)
Poultry (32%)
Red Meat (59%)

Source: U.S. Department of Agriculture

Question	Answer
1. What kind of meat was eaten the most by an average U.S. consumer in 1989?	___ Red meat ___ Poultry ___ Seafood
2. What kinds of meat did the average consumer in the U.S. eat more of in 1989 than in 1971? (Mark all that apply.)	___ Red meat ___ Poultry ___ Seafood
3. Finish this statement: About___ of the meat consumed in 1971 was either seafood or poultry.	___ 1/8 ___ 1/4 ___ 1/2
4. How much did poultry consumption increase between 1971 and 1989?	___ by about 10% ___ by about 20% ___ by about 30%
5. Martha is revising the recipe book she first published in the early 1970s. She wants to provide recipes that reflect what people like to eat. What should she do to revise her book?	___ increase the recipes that call for red meat ___ decrease the seafood recipes ___ increase the seafood and poultry recipes
6. During the 1980's, health awareness groups urged the American public to eat less red meat. Do the pie charts suggest this message got across to consumers?	___ Yes ___ No

5.16 Schedules: College, Appointment

5.16.1 College Class Schedule

Schedules tell when and where planned events or activities will take place.

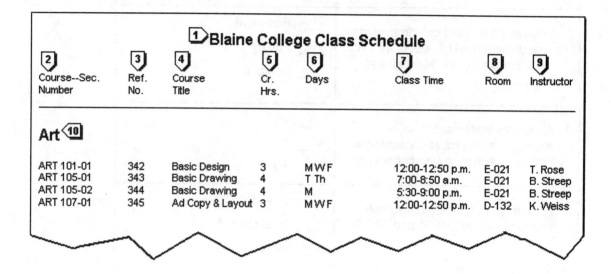

Blaine College Class Schedule

Course--Sec. Number	Ref. No.	Course Title	Cr. Hrs.	Days	Class Time	Room	Instructor
Art							
ART 101-01	342	Basic Design	3	M W F	12:00-12:50 p.m.	E-021	T. Rose
ART 105-01	343	Basic Drawing	4	T Th	7:00-8:50 a.m.	E-021	B. Streep
ART 105-02	344	Basic Drawing	4	M	5:30-9:00 p.m.	E-021	B. Streep
ART 107-01	345	Ad Copy & Layout	3	M W F	12:00-12:50 p.m.	D-132	K. Weiss

Understanding the Schedule

To learn more about the schedule above, refer to the number labels on the schedule and read the descriptions below.

 title

The title explains what a schedule is about generally. For example, this title says that the schedule shows classes that are offered at Blaine College. (This is part of the schedule.)

2 **Course--Sec. Number**

This column heading has the course section numbers of the art classes listed under it.

3 **Ref. No.**

This column heading has the reference numbers for each class listed under it.

4 **Course Title**

Under this column heading, the titles of each art course are listed.

5 **Cr. Hrs.**

The number of credit hours that each course is worth is listed underneath this column heading.

6 **Days**

The days that each class is offered are listed as abbreviations under this column heading. For example, "M" represents Monday.

7 **Class Time**

The times when the classes are offered are listed under this column heading.

8 **Room**

Under this column heading, the rooms where the classes are held are listed.

9 **Instructor**

The instructor for each class is listed under this column heading.

10 **Art**

This is the name of the department.

 **Check Your Understanding 5.16.1**

Refer to this schedule to answer the questions that follow. Put a check (✓) next to the correct answers in the answer column.

Blaine College Class Schedule

Course--Sec. Number	Ref. No.	Course Title	Cr. Hrs.	Days	Class Time	Room	Instructor
Art							
ART 101-01	342	Basic Design	3	M W F	12:00-12:50 p.m.	E-021	T. Rose
ART 105-01	343	Basic Drawing	4	T Th	7:00-8:50 a.m.	E-021	B. Streep
ART 105-02	344	Basic Drawing	4	M	5:30-9:00 p.m.	E-021	B. Streep
ART 107-01	345	Ad Copy & Layout	3	M W F	12:00-12:50 p.m.	D-132	K. Weiss

Question	Answer
1. The Ad Copy & Layout class will take place in which room?	___ 107-01 ___ 345 ___ D-132
2. At what time is the class that is only offered on Monday?	___ 12:00-12:50 p.m. ___ 5:30-9:00 p.m. ___ 7:00-8:50 a.m.
3. Who teaches the Basic Drawing class that is held on Tuesday and Thursday?	___ T. Rose ___ B. Streep ___ K. Weiss
4. If Monte wants to sign up for the Basic Drawing class on Mondays, which course number should he enter on his registration form?	___ ART 101-01 ___ ART 105-01 ___ ART 105-02
5. Lan needs four more credits to complete her graduation requirements. If she wants to take an art class, which should she take to give her the needed credits?	___ Basic Design ___ Basic Drawing ___ Ad Copy and Layout
6. Julia has a part-time job every Wednesday and Thursday afternoon from noon to 5:00 p.m. She wants to take as many art classes this semester as possible. Which classes can she fit in her schedule? (Mark all that apply.)	___ Basic Design ___ Basic Drawing ___ Ad Copy & Layout

5.16.2 Appointment Schedule

This schedule is a personal appointment schedule. It shows the times set aside to meet with specific people.

①Appointment Schedule
②

③

	Monday	Tuesday	Wednesday	Thursday	Friday
8 a.m.	Bill Jones				
9 a.m.		May Page	Chris Klein		
10 a.m.	Ed Gomez				Pete Hunt
11 a.m.					
Noon	Lunch		Lunch		Lunch
1 p.m.	Ben Stride	Lunch		Lunch	
2 p.m.	Lucy East				
3 p.m.		Carol Ong		Sandy Lee	
4 p.m.					

④

Understanding the Schedule

To learn more about the schedule, refer to the number labels on the schedule and read the descriptions below.

1 **title**

The title explains what a schedule is about generally. For example, this title says that this schedule shows appointments.

2 **days**

The days of the week are listed as column headings.

3 **time**

The times when appointments may be scheduled are listed as headings.

4 **appointments and activities**

The activities are listed in the schedule according to their appointment time (shown at the left of each row) and day (shown at the top of each column). For example, the appointment with Pete Hunt is on Friday at 10 a.m.

 **Check Your Understanding 5.16.2**

Refer to this schedule to answer the questions that follow. Put a check (✓) next to the correct answers in the answer column.

Appointment Schedule

	Monday	Tuesday	Wednesday	Thursday	Friday
8 a.m.	Bill Jones				
9 a.m.		May Page	Chris Klein		
10 a.m.	Ed Gomez				Pete Hunt
11 a.m.					
Noon	Lunch		Lunch		Lunch
1 p.m.	Ben Stride	Lunch		Lunch	
2 p.m.	Lucy East				
3 p.m.		Carol Ong		Sandy Lee	
4 p.m.					

Question	Answer
1. When is Carol Ong's appointment?	___ Monday, 2 p.m. ___ Tuesday, 3 p.m. ___ Thursday, 3 p.m.
2. Which day has the most appointments?	___ Monday ___ Tuesday ___ Friday
3. Which time slots are open for new appointments? (Mark all that apply.)	___ Wednesday, 1 p.m. ___ Monday, 2 p.m. ___ Thursday, 10 a.m. ___ Friday, noon
4. Are there more appointments scheduled for the mornings or for the afternoons?	___ mornings ___ afternoons
5. If Thursday has been blocked out of the schedule, on which days can Sandy Lee reschedule her appointment for the same hour? (Mark all that apply.)	___ Monday ___ Tuesday ___ Wednesday ___ Friday
6. Chris Klein needs to move his appointment to another day. He wants another 9:00 a.m. appointment, and he also wants to reserve two hours. Which day can he make his appointment?	___ Monday ___ Thursday ___ Friday

5.17 Schedules: Bus, Radio

5.17.1 Bus Schedule

Schedules tell when and where planned events or activities will take place. Bus schedules show what times of the day buses run, and where they stop.

Bus Schedule <1
Route 33
MONDAY - FRIDAY

OUTBOUND TO FOXWOOD <2   [3]

<4>

LEAVE Main St.	LEAVE Clifton Rd.	LEAVE Grayshon Dr.	LEAVE Coney St.	ARRIVE Foxwood Ave.
6:19am	6:21am	6:23am	6:27am	6:31am
6:47	6:49	6:51	6:56	7:01
7:10	7:12	7:14	7:17	7:21
7:17	7:20	7:23	7:25	7:29
7:44	7:46	7:48	7:53	7:58
7:51	7:53	7:55	8:00	8:05
8:07	8:09	8:11	8:16	8:21
8:32	8:34	8:36	8:41	8:46
9:52	9:54	9:56	10:01	10:06
10:50	10:52	10:54	10:59	11:04

Understanding the Schedule

To learn more about the schedule, refer to the number labels on the schedule and read the descriptions below.

1 **title**

The title explains what a schedule is about generally. For example, this title says that this schedule shows the route of bus #33 for Monday through Friday.

2 **subtitle**

The subtitle tells you this schedule is for the outbound bus that goes to Foxwood.

3 **bus stop**

The column headings show the places that bus #33 stops.

4 **time**

Each time listed on the schedule is the time that a #33 bus leaves the bus stop listed at the top of the column you are looking at. There are ten #33 buses listed on this schedule. The first one leaves 13 Main St. at 6:19 a.m. The last one leaves 13 Main St. at 10:50 a.m.

 **Check Your Understanding 5.17.1**

Refer to this schedule to answer the questions that follow. Put a check (✓) next to the correct answers in the answer column.

Bus Schedule
Route 33
MONDAY - FRIDAY

OUTBOUND TO FOXWOOD

LEAVE Main St.	LEAVE Clifton Rd.	LEAVE Grayshon Dr.	LEAVE Coney St.	ARRIVE Foxwood Ave.
6:19am	6:21am	6:23am	6:27am	6:31am
6:47	6:49	6:51	6:56	7:01
7:10	7:12	7:14	7:17	7:21
7:17	7:20	7:23	7:25	7:29
7:44	7:46	7:48	7:53	7:58
7:51	7:53	7:55	8:00	8:05
8:07	8:09	8:11	8:16	8:21
8:32	8:34	8:36	8:41	8:46
9:52	9:54	9:56	10:01	10:06
10:50	10:52	10:54	10:59	11:04

Question	Answer
1. What is the name of the fourth bus stop on this route?	___ Grayshon Drive ___ Coney St. ___ Foxwood Ave.
2. What time does the third bus of the day leave Grayshon Drive?	___ 7:10 a.m. ___ 6:23 a.m. ___ 7:14 a.m.
3. What time does the last bus reach Foxwood Ave.?	___ 10:50 a.m. ___ 11:04 a.m. ___ 11:54 a.m.
4. About how long after the first bus to Foxwood leaves Main Street does the second bus leave?	___ about 20 minutes later ___ about 30 minutes later ___ about 40 minutes later
5. Tameeka has an appointment near Coney St. at 10:00 a.m. What bus should she take from Main Street to make sure she arrives at her appointment at least 30 minutes early?	___ the 8:07 bus ___ the 8:32 bus ___ the 9:52 bus
6. Chester must arrive at work on Foxwood Ave. no later than 8:00 a.m. What is the latest bus he can take from Clifton Rd. that will get him to work on time?	___ the 7:12 bus ___ the 7:46 bus ___ the 7:48 bus

5.17.2 Radio Schedule

This schedule shows the weekly program times for a radio station.

WBCC PROGRAM SCHEDULE 1

3	SUN.	MON.	TUES.	WED.	THU.	FRI.	SAT.	
7:00	MORNING WAKE-UP		4 BREAKFAST JAM				SWEET AND BLUE	7:00
8:00	RADIO VENEX						JAMMER	8:00
9:00		REACH OUT EARTH		FOLK'S THE GAME		ALIVE	REGGAE RUNNIN'	9:00
10:00	YOUR CHOICE	ART CHAT		ALL IN THE NEWS		TAKE-2	MOLDY OLDIES	10:00
11:00								11:00

Understanding the Schedule

To learn more about the schedule, refer to the number labels on the schedule and read the descriptions below.

1 **title**

The title explains what a schedule is about generally. For example, this title says that this schedule shows the program schedule for WBCC.

2 **days of the week**

The days of the week when programs are broadcast are listed as column headings. For example, the program called Jammer is on Saturday.

3 **time**

The time when each program airs is listed in the far left and far right columns of the schedule. For example, the program called Reggae Runnin' airs at 9:00 a.m.

4 **programs**

The names of the radio programs are shown in the main body of the schedule.

 **Check Your Understanding 5.17.2**

Refer to this schedule to answer the questions that follow. Put a check (✓) next to the correct answers in the answer column.

WBCC PROGRAM SCHEDULE

	SUN.	MON.	TUES.	WED.	THU.	FRI.	SAT.	
7:00	MORNING WAKE-UP	BREAKFAST JAM					SWEET AND BLUE	7:00
8:00	RADIO VENEX						JAMMER	8:00
9:00		REACH OUT EARTH		FOLK'S THE GAME		ALIVE	REGGAE RUNNIN'	9:00
10:00	YOUR CHOICE	ART CHAT		ALL IN THE NEWS		TAKE- 2	MOLDY OLDIES	10:00
11:00								11:00

Question	Answer
1. What radio program is on at 9 a.m. on Wednesday?	___ *All in the News* ___ *Breakfast Jam* ___ *Folk's the Game*
2. What time does the program *Sweet and Blue* finish?	___ 8:00 a.m. ___ 7:00 a.m. ___ 9:00 a.m.
3. Which radio program gets the most air time — is on the most often?	___ *Reach Out Earth* ___ *All in the News* ___ *Breakfast Jam*
4. Which program is on for two hours on Sundays?	___ *Morning Wake-up* ___ *Radio Venex* ___ *Reach Out Earth*
5. Howard loves Reggae music and basketball. He doesn't want to miss his favorite radio program, *Reggae Runnin'*. When should he tell his friends he can play basketball on Saturday mornings?	___ before 9:00 a.m. or after 10:00 a.m. ___ before 10:00 a.m. or after 11:00 a.m. ___ before 8:00 a.m. or after 9:00 a.m.
6. Gisela is planning to teach a class on Mondays, Wednesdays, and Fridays from 9:00 to 10:00 a.m. Will she be able to continue listening to her favorite radio program, *TAKE-2*?	___ Yes ___ No

5.18 Tables: Minerals, Movies

5.18.1 Minerals: Source and Use in the Body

This table shows the food sources of minerals, and how the human body uses these minerals.

① **Minerals — Source and Use in the Body**

② MINERALS	③ NEEDED FOR	④ SOURCES
⑤ Calcium	strong teeth and bones; blood clotting; heart and nerve action	meat, milk, vegetables, fruit, and bread
Iodine	proper functioning of thyroid gland	seafood and iodized salt
Iron	red blood cell production	liver, lean meats, shellfish, green leafy vegetables, whole grains
Magnesium	nerve and muscle action	whole grains and vegetables
Phosphorus	strong teeth and bones; making ATP	meat, milk, vegetables, fruit, bread, and cereal
Potassium	body growth; cell and blood activities	fruits and vegetables
Sodium	blood and body tissues	table salt and vegetables
Zinc	enzyme production	protein foods

Understanding the Table

To learn more about the table, refer to the number labels on the table and read the descriptions below.

1> title

This is the title. It gives you a general idea of what the table is about. This title tells you that the table is about sources and uses of minerals in the body.

2> Minerals

This column lists different types of minerals needed by the body.

3> Needed for

This column lists the reasons why the body needs minerals.

4> Sources

This column lists the food sources of minerals.

5> row

In this table, each row gives information for a particular mineral. For example, the first row on the table gives this information for calcium.

 **Check Your Understanding 5.18.1**

Refer to this table to answer the questions that follow. Put a check (✓) next to the correct answers in the answer column.

Minerals — Source and Use in the Body

MINERALS	NEEDED FOR	SOURCES
Calcium	strong teeth and bones; blood clotting; heart and nerve action	meat, milk, vegetables, fruit, and bread
Iodine	proper functioning of thyroid gland	seafood and iodized salt
Iron	red blood cell production	liver, lean meats, shellfish, green leafy vegetables, whole grains
Magnesium	nerve and muscle action	whole grains and vegetables
Phosphorus	strong teeth and bones; making ATP	meat, milk, vegetables, fruit, bread, and cereal
Potassium	body growth; cell and blood activities	fruits and vegetables
Sodium	blood and body tissues	table salt and vegetables
Zinc	enzyme production	protein foods

Question	Answer
1. What mineral is needed for red blood cell production?	___ zinc ___ iron ___ iodine
2. The foods where minerals are found are discussed under the column heading	___ Minerals ___ Needed For ___ Sources
3. What foods are rich sources of calcium? (Mark all that apply.)	___ meat ___ milk ___ table salt ___ vegetables
4. ATP is a substance found in the muscles that helps your muscles contract. Which mineral does your body need to make ATP?	___ zinc ___ phosphorus ___ calcium
5. Which minerals help strengthen the bones? (Mark all that apply.)	___ calcium ___ iodine ___ phosphorus ___ zinc
6. What mineral is needed for the proper functioning of the thyroid gland?	___ phosphorus ___ iron ___ iodine

5.18.2 Motion Picture Theaters: Average Admission Price and Attendance

This table shows information about theater admission price and attendance for three different years.

1 **U.S. Motion Picture Theaters:
Average Admission Price and Attendance,
1970, 1980, 1990**

4

	1970	1980	1990
2 Admission Avg. Price (dollars)	1.55	2.69	4.75
3 Attendance (millions)	921	1,022	1,058

5 Source: Motion Picture Association of America, Inc., New York, NY

Understanding the Table

To learn more about the table, refer to the number labels on the table and read the descriptions below.

1 **title**

The title gives you a general idea of what the table is about. This title tells you that the table shows the average price and attendance at U.S. motion picture theaters in 1970, 1980, and 1990.

2 **Admission Avg. Price (dollars)**

This row title tells you that the numbers in the row show the average admission price in dollars.

3 **Attendance**

This row title informs you that the numbers in the row show the attendance in millions. For example, the attendance in 1970 was 921 million or 921,000,000.

4 **date**

The dates along the top of the table are column headings. The numbers listed under each heading show information for each year.

5 **Source: Motion Picture Association of America, Inc., New York, NY**

This is the source of the information shown in the chart.

Check Your Understanding 5.18.2

Refer to this table to answer the questions that follow. Put a check (✓) next to the correct answers in the answer column.

U.S. Motion Picture Theaters:
Average Admission Price and Attendance,
1970, 1980, 1990

	1970	1980	1990
Admission Avg. Price (dollars)	1.55	2.69	4.75
Attendance (millions)	921	1,022	1,058

Source: Motion Picture Association of America, Inc., New York, NY

Question	Answer
1. What was the average admission price in 1970?	___ $1.55 ___ $2.69 ___ $4.75
2. In what year was the theater attendance 1,022,000,000?	___ 1970 ___ 1980 ___ 1990
3. How much did the average price of going to a movie increase between 1970 and 1980?	___ about $1.00 ___ about $2.00 ___ about $3.00
4. How much did movie attendance increase between 1980 and 1990?	___ about 20 million ___ about 30 million ___ about 40 million
5. If the price of going to a movie increases as much in the next ten years as it did between 1980 and 1990, how much will you pay to go to a movie by the year 2000?	___ around $4.75 ___ around $5.75 ___ around $6.75
6. If movie attendance increases as much in the next ten years as it did between 1980 and 1990, how many millions of people will attend movies in the year 2000?	___ 1,094,000,000 ___ 1,022,000,000 ___ 921,000,000

5.19 Answers to Questions

Answers to 5.1.1

Correct Answer	Explanation
1. $5.10	Look at the price listed at the end of the *Italy* bar. Italy has the most expensive gasoline, $5.10 per gallon.
2. Japan	Look for the price that is closest to $4.00. Then look at the bar's label to see that the bar represents the price in Japan.
3. Canada	Look for the bar closest in length to the *U.S.* bar. Notice that Canada's bar is closest in length. The U.S. price is $1.43 per gallon and the Canadian price is $2.06 per gallon.
4. United Kingdom and Germany	Look for the two bars on the graph that are closest in length. The bars for the United Kingdom and Germany appear to be closest in length. The price in Germany ($2.87) is only 32 cents more than the price in the United Kingdom ($2.55).
5. United Kingdom	Compare the bars for the countries listed. Locate the shortest bar. The United Kingdom has the least expensive gasoline costs per gallon of the countries listed in this question.
6. Venezuela	Venezuela's price is much less than all the others. Gas is probably cheaper there because Venezuela must produce all or most of its own petroleum. Therefore, the cost is much lower.

Answers to 5.1.2

Correct Answer	Explanation
1. 88%	Between 1992 and 2005 the number of physical therapist jobs is forecast to grow by 88%. (Note: Make sure you looked at the physical therapists bar, not the bar for physical therapy assistants.)
2. Computer Engineers	The number of computer engineering jobs is forecast to grow by 112% between 1992 and 2005.
3. 86%	Locate the paralegal bar and look at the percent label at the end of the bar. You could expect an increase of 86%.
4. Medicine/Health Care	Count the number of bars that fall into each category. There are at least four in the medicine/health care category: medical assistants, physical therapists, physical therapy assistants, and home health aides (you might also count personal and home care aides). There are two bars in the computers category: systems analysts and computer engineers. In the teaching category there is only one bar: special ed. teachers.
5. 110%	Look for the systems analyst bar and notice the percent increase (110%).
6. Home Health Aide	First locate the bars for the occupations listed. Notice that the number of Home Health Aides is projected to increase the most (138%) in the future. So Charles should consider this occupation if he wants a career in health care with the most job opportunities.

Answers to 5.2.1

Correct Answer	Explanation
1. bicycle, subway and train	The number of people using bicycles, the subway, or trains to get to work decreased by only 0.1%. This is the smallest percent on the graph.
2. 1.1%	Look for the bus bar and read its value. The number of people riding the bus to work decreased by 1.1%.
3. Positive percents represent increases; negative percents indicate decreases. The longest bar shows the greatest % change; the shortest bar shows the least % change.	This is a correct assumption. The positive percents are above the axis, showing an increase. Negative percents are below the axis, showing a decrease. This is a correct assumption. The longer the bar the greater the percent change. (Note: The other assumption listed is NOT a correct assumption because the bars do not represent total numbers of people. The bars represent percent change.)
4. The number of people riding the train to work decreased by 0.1% in 1980.	The number of people riding the train to work decreased by 0.1% BETWEEN 1980 and 1990, not in 1980.
5. less	The bars representing public transportation (bus, subway, train) are negative. This means people used public transportation less during the 1980s.
6. No	Look for the drive alone bar. Notice that it shows the largest increase (8.8%). So even with the ad campaign, driving alone has increased, not decreased, over the past ten years.

Answers to 5.2.2

Correct Answer	Explanation
1. coffee, roasted	The price of these four food items changed as shown below: roasted coffee decreased by 27% whole wheat bread increased 24% fresh, whole milk increased 23% ground beef increased 19% The percent change for coffee was the largest of these food items.
2. 30%	Look for the percent shown above the tomato bar. The price of tomatoes increased by 30%.
3. The axis (horizontal line) represents no change in the price. The bars below the axis show a decrease in price; bars above the axis show an increase in price.	This is a correct assumption. The axis represents zero, or no change. This is a correct assumption. The positive percents are above the axis, showing an increase. Negative percents are below the axis, showing a decrease. (Note: The statement that the bars represent the actual prices is not true. The bars show a percent change in the cost. You cannot tell what the actual costs were from this graph.)
4. The price of coffee increased by 27%.	The *Coffee, roasted* bar has -27% next to it. This means the price of coffee DECREASED by 27%.
5. bread, whole wheat	The graph shows that the price for bread increased 24%. Therefore, it was cheaper in 1986 than in 1992. The other two items shown, shortening and coffee, actually decreased in cost over the same period.
6. 19%	The graph shows the price of ground beef increased 19% between 1986 and 1992. To keep making a profit, the manager will have to increase the price of his hamburgers by a minimum of 19% in order to cover the increased cost of ground beef.

Answers to 5.3.1

Correct Answer	Explanation
1. 230	Notice the *Bird* bar appears to reach about half way between the 200 and 250 grid lines. So 230 seems to be the best answer.
2. Plants	The category with the most threatened species is represented by the longest threatened species bar (■). The *Plants* group has the longest threatened species bar; it represents approximately 75 species.
3. fewer	Find and compare the endangered species bars for birds and mammals. Notice that the *Bird* endangered species bar represents 250 species and the *Mammals* bar represents 310 species.
4. 3 times	Compare the endangered species bars for clams and insects. Notice the *Clam* bar is about 3 times as long.
5. almost 300	The *Plant* endangered species bar (▢) reaches more than halfway between the 250 and 300 grid lines. So it would be fair to say that there are almost 300 endangered plant species.
4. 75	The *Reptile* endangered species bar (▢) reaches about halfway between the 50 and 100 grid lines. So there are around 75 different reptile endangered species.

Answers to 5.3.2

Correct Answer	Explanation
1. radio sets	Look at the longest bar for 1980. It is found in the *Radio Sets* category.
2. VCRs	Compare the pairs of bars representing 1980 and 1992. Find the pair that has the biggest difference. It is found in the *VCR* category. This category had the largest percent change between 1980 and 1992.
3. 70%	Find the 1992 *VCR* bar and notice which grid line it almost reaches (70%).
4. 4	Notice that the 1980 *Cable TV* bar reaches about 15% and the 1992 bar reaches about 60%. So the 1992 bar is about four times as long as the 1980 bar.
5. around 90%	Find the 1992 *Telephone Service* bar. Notice that it's closest to the 90% griddle.
3. almost 60%	Look at the 1992 bar for cable TV. Notice that it reaches about halfway between the 50% and 60% grid lines. So almost 60% of the households would have to pay the cable TV tax.

Answers to 5.4.1

Correct Answer	Explanation
1. 1985	*The Field of Social Work* was published in 1985. (Note: To quickly locate book titles look for words in italics.)
2. Garth Alpenstein and others	Journal articles appear in quotation marks. Garth Alpenstein and others authored the journal article "Health Problems of Homeless Children in New York City."
3. *The Field of Social Work*	Look for the numbers near the *ed.* notation in the bibliography entries. Notice that *The Field of Social Work* is in its 8th edition.
4. Harper	Look for the entry for *The American Red Cross: The First Century*. Then notice the publisher just before the copyright date.
5. *Juvenile Justice in America*	Look for the most recent publication date at the end of each source listed. This book by Simonsen is the most recent source listed in the bibliography (1991).
6. Alpenstein, Garth and others Kozol, Jonathan	Look for book titles that mention children. The sources by Alpenstein and Kozol, "Health Problems of Homeless Children in New York City" and *Rachel and Her Children: Homeless Families in America*, would be useful to learn more about homeless children.

Answers to 5.4.2

Correct Answer	Explanation
1. New York	*Figure Painting In Watercolors* was published in New York.
2. Watson-Guptill	Watson-Guptill are the publishers of *A Complete Guide to Watercolor Painting*.
3. Prentice Hall, Englewood Cliffs, New Jersey	Look for the publisher of the book listed. You can usually call the publisher to find out where to purchase a book. Sometimes you can order directly from the publisher.
4. *Watercolor Day by Day*	Look for the book with the most recent publication date. The most recent source, *Watercolor Day by Day*, was published in 1987.
5. Taubes	The book by Taubes, *The Painter's Dictionary of Materials and Methods*, seems to be a ready reference source for looking up terms related to watercolor painting.
6. Gaunt	The book by Gaunt, *The March of the Moderns*, sounds like a good resource to use to learn more about modern watercolor painters.

Answers to 5.5.1

Correct Answer	Explanation
1. Wednesdays	The "W" in front of the time means that the course is held on Wednesday.
2. 4	This course is worth 4 hours of credit.
3. $40	Notice this class has a $40 special fee.
4. Yes	The description says that this is "an introductory course in video production." If it were important to have prerequisite skills, these skills or experience should be listed. So it appears to be okay to take the class without any prior experience.
5. creating special effects	Look to see which of these skills is mentioned in the course description. Notice that "creating special effects" was not mentioned.
6. 10	You know the class starts on Feb. 28 and ends on May 1. So there are two class sessions. Then there are probably about eight other classes between these two times, assuming there are usually four Wednesdays each in March and April.

Answers to 5.5.2

Correct Answer	Explanation
1. $12.00	The list price for the 100-page photo album is $12.00.
2. $0.31	A customer saves $0.31 when a refill is purchased.
3. 0398-1239	Look for the order number that goes with the 100-page album. It's important to make sure you have the right number. Because if you make a mistake, the company will send you the wrong item.
4. No	Carefully read the description of the magnetic photo album. Notice what type of cover it has. This photo album has a vinyl cover, not a leather one like Phuong wants.
5. 4	There are 25 pages per refill. So you would need to buy four refills to double the number of pages in the original 100-page album.
6. $7.00	Look under the *Our Price* column to find the cost of the album (about $6.00). Then look under the same column to find the cost of the refill (about $1.00). So the total cost would be about $7.00.

Answers to 5.6.1

Correct Answer	Explanation
1. Los Angeles International	Los Angeles International Airport was the third busiest airport in 1991 when the ranking is made based on the number of paying passengers boarding at the airport.
2. 9,737,000	Find the number under the *Paying Passengers Boarding* column for Newark International Airport (9,737). Each figure on the chart must be multiplied by 1,000. So, the number of paying passengers that boarded aircraft at Newark International Airport in 1991 was 9,737,000.
3. Newark International	Find the smallest number listed under the *Aircraft Departures* column (128). Then see which airport this number belongs to (Newark International). (Note: You can't use rank to find this number, because rank is based on the number of paying passengers boarding at the airport.)
4. 145,000	Look for the number of planes leaving the airport under the *Aircraft Departures* column for Phoenix Sky Harbor International (145). This number is shown in thousands; so it needs to be multiplied by 1,000.
5. 9,352,000	To get on the top ten list, an airport probably needs to have more passengers boarding than at least the 10th busiest airport. So look for the airport ranked tenth (St. Louis International). Then note how many passengers board at this airport (about 9,352). This number is in thousands so you have to multiply by 1,000. You get 9,352,000.

6. Chicago, O'Hare	Notice that the Chicago, O'Hare airport is ranked as the number one busiest airport. It has the most aircraft departures and paying passengers boarding there. So it's probably best to avoid routing vacation travelers through this airport where possible.

Answers to 5.6.2

Correct Answer	Explanation
1. 4,662 miles	Find a row heading for Moscow and a column heading for New York. Then follow across the column and down the row until you pinpoint the cell where the row and column meet. Moscow is 4,662 miles from New York.
2. Tokyo	Look for a box (cell) that says 6,033. Then follow the column up to the top of the chart and read the column heading. Next follow the row across the chart and read the row heading. You see that this is the distance from Tokyo to Paris. Tokyo is 6,033 miles from Paris.
3. New York	Find the row for Darwin. Then look across the row until you find the largest number (9,959). Look up at the column heading for this number (New York). New York is the greatest distance from Darwin, 9,959 miles.

4. New York Tokyo, Japan	Find the row for Moscow. Look across the row until you find any numbers that are close to one another. Look at the column headings and see which cities these numbers belong to. Then look for these cities in the answer options. New York is 4,662 miles from Moscow. Tokyo, Japan is 4,650 miles from Moscow. There is a difference of only 12 miles.

5. London, England
   Moscow, Russia
   Paris, France
	Look for the New York City row. Look across this row and note any numbers that are less than 5,000 miles. Look up at the column headings and see which cities these numbers belong to.

6. 11,000 miles	Find the distance between New York City and Mexico City (2,085), Mexico City and London, (5,541), and London and New York City (3,459). Then add these numbers and you can see they add up to about 11,000 miles.

Answers to 5.7.1

Correct Answer	Explanation
1. 7	Look under the *Description* column for "moderate gale." Then look under the *Number* column to see what number is used with a moderate gale. The wind scale number of a moderate gale is 7.
2. 19-24 miles per hour	Look for the *fresh breeze* row and then under the *Speed* column. During a fresh breeze the wind speed is 19-24 miles per hour.
3. Widespread damage	Look under the *Number* column and find 11. Then look under the *Characteristics* column. A force 11 wind causes widespread damage.

4. No	Look under the *Number* column and find the *1* row. Look at the wind speed for this number (1-3 mph). Oriana's kite flies best in 8-10 mph winds. So she shouldn't plan to fly her kite. There probably won't be enough wind.
5. Yes	Look up *fresh gale* under the *Description* column. Then look for the wind speed that goes with this description (39-46 mph). This exceeds Stuart's limit (30 mph). Stuart better return to the dock to keep safe.
6. No	Look for the hurricane wind speed on the chart. Notice it says 74 miles per hour and above. So Hector should not expect these shutters to last through a hurricane.

Answers to 5.7.2

Correct Answer	Explanation
1. 27°C	Look across the *Deciduous Forest* row under the *Average Temperature* column heading. In a deciduous forest, the average high temperature is 27°C.
2. rain forest	Find the cell that says 9-12 months. Then look across to the row heading. Rain forests have a growing season length of 9-12 months.
3. coniferous forest	Look under the Average Rainfall column and find the lowest number range (25-125 cm). Then look across at the row heading for this amount of rain. Notice it is the coniferous forest.

4. coniferous forests	Look down the Growing Season column until you find the shortest range of months (2-5 months). Then look across the row and see what type of forest has this length of growing season (coniferous forest). You know Alaska has only several months' growing season; so it must have mostly coniferous forests.
5. 75-125 cm	You need to find the rainfall for broadleaf trees, because you are talking about oak and beech trees. Look for the row heading that includes broadleaf trees (*Deciduous forest*). Then look under the *Average Rainfall Per Year* column. Notice the rainfall is 75-125 cm. So most likely the average yearly rainfall in the Black Forest is in this range.
6. 25°C to 35°C	The key word is *tropical*. Look for tropical mentioned on the *Type of Forest* column. It mentions *tropical* under the *Rain Forest* category. If Omar bought a tropical plant, it would most likely survive under rain forest temperature conditions. So look on the chart to find the average temperature range for rain forests (25°C to 35°C).

Answers to 5.8.1

Correct Answer	Explanation
1. Feb. '95	Find $2,000 under the *Fund-raising Goals* column. Then look across this row under the *Target Date* column. Notice Feb. '95 is the target date to raise $2,000.
2. Oct. '95	Look under the *Fund-raising Goals* column to find $6,000. Then look across under the *Actual Date Goal Reached* column. Notice that by Oct. '95, $6,000 was raised for the animal shelter.

3. $2,000	Look under the *Actual Date Goal Reached* column. Find Jul. '95 and Oct. '95. Then look across the row for each of these numbers and see which goal was reached on each date. By Jul. '95 the committee had raised $4,000 and they had reached $6,000 by Oct. To find the amount raised between Jul. and Oct. subtract $4,000 from $6,000. You get $2,000.
4. 10 months	Look under the *Target Date to Reach Goal* column. Find the first goal date, starting at the bottom of the chart (Feb. '95). Then find the last goal date (Nov. '95) at the top of the chart. Count how many months there are from Feb. to Nov. (10).
5. 10 months	Look under the *Actual Date Goal Reached* column. Find the first goal date, starting at the bottom of the chart (Jan. '95). Then find the last goal date (Oct. '95) at the top of the chart. Count how many months there are from Jan. to Oct. (10).
6. Jan., Jul., Oct.	The fund-raising committee should make last year's actual dates the target dates for the coming year.

Answers to 5.8.2

Correct Answer	Explanation
1. 150 calories	Notice that under the section of the label called *Amount Per Serving*, you see a heading called *Calories*. There it says 150 calories per serving. But how big is a serving? Look at the top of the label under the heading *Nutrition Facts*. Notice it lists the serving size as 4 cookies. So you know there are 150 calories in four chocolate mint cookies. (Note: *Calories from Fat* lets you know that of the 150 calories you get from the cookies, 70 of those calories come from the fat in the cookies.)

2. 25%	Look under the *% Daily Value* section of the chart. Find the row that says *Saturated Fat* and look across and see what % is listed under the *% Daily Value* column. Four chocolate mint cookies contain 25% of the daily intake of saturated fat. This is based on a 2,000 calorie diet.
3. 16	You already know that one serving of cookies gives you 25% of your daily saturated fat intake. You also know this is based on one serving of cookies, or four cookies. So if four cookies give you 25% of your daily amount. Then four times four cookies will give you 100% of your daily saturated fat.
4. chocolate mint cookies	To see if there is any sodium in these cookies, find the *Sodium* row and check the amount of sodium. It says there is 70mg of sodium in a 28g serving of the chocolate mint cookies. If Homer wants to buy the cookies with less sodium he should buy the chocolate mint cookies.
5. No	Check to see if there is any cholesterol in the cookies. Under the *% Daily Value* section it says there is 0%. So these cookies do not contain cholesterol.
6. 375g	Karen's above-average physical activity means she requires more than the usual 2,000 calorie daily intake. It's more likely that her needs are shown under the 2,500 calorie column on the reference value chart. So her total carbohydrate intake should be in the 375g-per-day range.

Answers to 5.9.1

Correct Answer	Explanation
1. 880,000	Look under the *Age* column to find the 55-64 heading. Then look across this row until you are under the *Numbers* column. Notice it says 880. The numbers in this column are in thousands. So you multiply the number you found by 1,000. The number of workers age 55-64 on flexible schedules was 880,000 in 1991.
2. 35-44	Look under the *Percent* column until you find 16.5%. Then look across the row and note the heading. The 35-44 age group had 16.5% of its workers on a flexible schedule in 1991.
3. 25-34	Look under the *Number* column and find the largest number (4,008). Then look across the row for the heading. Notice this number belongs to the 25-34 age group. This age group had the greatest number of workers on flexible schedules.
4. 16-19	Look under the *Percent* column and find the smallest percent (10.6%). Then look across the row for the heading. Notice this percent belongs to the 16-19 age group. This age group had the smallest percent of its workers on flexible schedules.
5. 3,591,000	Find the number of workers on flexible schedules for the 35-44 age group (3,744) and the 65+ age group (153). Subtract the smaller number from the larger number. You get about 3,591. This number is in thousands; so you multiply by 1,000 to get 3,591,000.
6. 25-34, 35-44	The chart shows that the two groups with the greatest number of workers on flexible schedules are the 25-34 group with 4,008,000 workers and the 35-44 group with 3,744,000 workers.

Answers to 5.9.2

Correct Answer	Explanation
1. 2,104,000	Find the *Car dealers* row and look under the *Employees* column. Notice the number given is 2,104. The numbers under this column are in thousands. So, in 1990 the number of employees of automotive dealers and service stations was 2,104,000.
2. Furniture and home furnishings stores	Find 11.8 under the *Payroll 1989* column. Then look across the row for the heading that goes with this number. *Furniture and home furnishings stores* had a payroll of $11.8 billion in 1989.
3. 108,100	Look under the Businesses 1990 column for furniture and home furnishing stores. Notice you see the number 108.1. This number is shown in thousands. Multiply by 1,000 to get the actual number. There were 108,100 furniture and home furnishing stores in 1990.
4. Car dealers and service stations	Compare the numbers in the 1989 and 1990 columns under the *Employees* heading. Notice if any of the numbers decrease in 1990 instead of increasing. The number of car dealers and service station employees decreased between 1989 and 1990.
5. General merchandise stores	Look under the *Businesses 1990* column for the three categories listed. Which category has the smallest number? The general merchandise stores had the fewest number of stores in 1990 (36,000).

| 6. Eating and drinking places | Compare the payroll numbers for each industry between 1989 and 1990.

Notice the payroll numbers increased the most for the *eating and drinking places* industry. The payroll for this industry increased 3.5 billion in one year. |
|---|---|

Answers to 5.10.1

Correct Answer	Explanation
1. U.S. companies	In 1991, more bikes were sold by U.S. companies. The line showing domestic shipments (▫—▫) was higher than the line for imports (●—●) that year.
2. approximately 6 million	Look for the domestic shipments line above the 1990 mark. Then trace across the graph with your finger and see that this point matches up with the six on the *Millions of Bikes Sold* axis (vertical line).

In 1990, U.S. companies sold approximately 6 million bikes. |
| 3. 1987 | Look for the highest point the reached by the imports line (●—●). Then trace your finger down to the bottom of the graph to see what year this goes with.

The highest point for foreign bike sales was 1987. |
| 4. the year after foreign bike sales reached their highest point | Find the domestic shipments line (▫—▫) and trace along it until you find its lowest point. Then look down and see which year goes with this point. Was this the year before or after foreign sales peaked?

It was the year after foreign sales peaked (1988). |

| 5. about 3 million | Find the end point of each line above the 1991 mark. Then trace across from both points to the vertical axis (*Millions of bikes sold* line) and look for the closest number that goes with each line.

(Note: You might want to hold up a piece of paper to help you line up the points with the vertical axis.)

The last point of the domestic shipment line (▫—▫) reaches to about the 7 million level and the import line (●—●) is closer to the 4 million level. So, 7 million minus 4 million equals about 3 million. The U.S. companies sold 3 million more bikes than the foreign companies in 1991. |
| 6. between 1980-85 | Watch what happens to the foreign imports line between each set of year marks. Between which marks does the line go up the most sharply?

The imports line goes up the most sharply between the 1980 and 1985 marks. |

Answers to 5.10.2

Correct Answer	Explanation
1. Grades K-8	The category that consistently had the most students enrolled during 1970 to 1990 was Grades K-8. The line for this category (⁻·●·⁻) is higher than the lines for Grades 9-12 and College.
2. College	Between 1970 and 1980, the enrollment of students in colleges increased. This is shown on the graph by a rising line (⁻◇⁻).
3. Grades K-8	Look for the line that went down between 1970 and 1980. It was the Grades K-8 line (⁻·●·⁻).

4. Grades 9-12, College	Look for the lines that are nearest to each other by the year 2000. The Grades 9-12 line (—▲—) and the College line (-◇-) are about at the same level by the year 2000.
5. about 25 million more	Look for the Grades K-8 line (-·●·-) and the Grades 9-12 line (—▲—) above the year 2000 mark. Hold up a piece of paper or use your finger to trace across to the vertical axis (*Millions of students enrolled* line) from each point. Guess the approximate level each line reaches. The K-8 line reaches about the 40 million level and the Grades 9-12 line reaches about the 15 million level. When you subtract 15 from 40 you get 25. So there will be about 25 million more students enrolled in Grades K-8 than in Grades 9-12 in the year 2000.
6. 10 million more	Look at the Total Enrollment line (-·■·-). Where does it reach for 1990? (approximately 60 million) Where does it reach for 2000? (approximately 70 million) There will be about 10 million more students enrolled in the year 2000 than in 1990.

Answers to 5.11.1

Correct Answer	Explanation
1. 2nd Ave.	Find the library symbol in the key. Then locate the library on the map. What is the street label for the street where the library is located? The library is located on 2nd Ave.
2. city hall	Locate the hospital on the map. Then look at the compass to see which way is north on the map. Next look for the building immediately north of the hospital. Find the symbol in the key to identify the building. The city hall is immediately north of the hospital.

3. Union Ave. and 1st Ave.	To get from the school to the hospital, you would go down Union Ave. and 1st Ave. (Note: You could also go down 2nd Ave. and Main Street.)
4. one block	Locate the city hall and the post office on the map. Then look to see about how many blocks one is from the other. They're about one block from each other.
5. west	Find the hospital and the city park. Look at the compass to find directions on the map. Then decide which direction the park is from the hospital. The park is west of the hospital.
6. School	Locate in your mind where the new park would be found. Then compare the locations of the three buildings listed. The new park would be nearer to the school than to any of the other buildings listed.

Answers to 5.11.2

Correct Answer	Explanation
1. west side	Refer to the compass to see the directions on the map. The road is located on the west side of the lake.
2. 4	Count the picnic table symbols on the map. There are four picnic areas.
3. trail	Refer to the key to see what the smallest dotted line represents. The smallest dotted line on the map represents a trail.

4. Southwest and Northeast	Look at the compass to note directions on the map. Then locate the nature walks. Decide which direction the walks are located from the lake. One nature walk is located southwest of the lake and the other northeast of the lake.
5. east	Find the side of the lake where there are no picnic areas. Refer to the compass to decide on the direction. There are no picnic areas east of the lake.
6. Probably not	Compare the distance covered by the walk around the lake and the two nature walks. Don't be afraid to use your fingers to measure. It appears that the two nature walks together approximately equal the distance around the lake. So it would probably take about double the time to walk around the lake and do the nature walks as well. Therefore, having only an extra 15 minutes to do the whole walk in an hour and a half is not realistic.

Answers to 5.12.1

Correct Answer	Explanation
1. 339 miles	Look at the line connecting Denver and Durango and read the number between the lines. Durango is 339 miles from Denver.
2. Denver	Compare the distance shown between Grand Junction and the three places listed. Grand Junction is closest to Denver, which is 246 miles away.

3. Grand Junction	Find Craig first. Then check the distances from Craig to each of the locations listed. Look for the shortest distance. Craig is closest to Grand Junction, which is 153 miles away.
4. Durango	First find Denver. Then check the distances from Denver to each of the locations listed. Look for the longest distance. Durango is furthest from Denver.
5. 340 miles	Look at the distance between Durango and Grand Junction (170 miles). If Derek rides to Grand Junction and back, the total distance will be 2 x 170 or about 340 miles.
6. Denver, Grand Junction, Pueblo, Denver	Add up the mileages for each route. Then compare your number and decide which route is shorter. You find that the visiting Pueblo via Grand Junction is 80 miles shorter than visiting Pueblo via Durango.

Answers to 5.12.2

Correct Answer	Explanation
1. 10-15 million	Look for Illinois on the map by locating the state with the IL abbreviation. Note the pattern used to fill in the state. Then refer to the key and see what population range this pattern matches. In 1990, the population of Illinois was 10-15 million.
2. North Carolina (NC) and Michigan (MI)	Refer to the key to find out which pattern was used to fill in states with 5-20 million people. Then locate the states listed and see which ones are filled with this pattern. North Carolina (NC) and Michigan (MI) both had populations of 5-10 million in 1990.

3. 6	Look on the key for the color used to show populations less than 1 million. Then count the number of states that show this color. There were 6 states with populations less than 1 million in 1990, Alaska (AK), Montana (MT), Wyoming (WY), North Dakota (ND), South Dakota (SD), and Vermont (VT).
4. eastern half	Find all the states that have between 5-10 million populations. Where are they found? All these states are found in the eastern half of the United States.
5. Pennsylvania (PA)	Refer to the map to find out which of the states listed has the largest population. This state will have the most representatives in the U.S. House of Representatives. The state in the list with the most representatives is Pennsylvania, because it has the largest population.
6. New York, (NY), California (CA), Texas (TX)	Refer to the key to find the color used to show the states with the largest populations (>15 million). Then find all states that color. The publisher should make sure and check the requirements of New York, California, and Texas.

Answers to 5.13.1

Correct Answer	Explanation
1. Hancock Building	Find the number of the building nearest the parking lot and then look up its name in the key. The building nearest to the parking lot is building number 5, the Hancock Building.

2. Jay Memorial Building	Use the compass to find directions on the chart. The Piker Fieldhouse is building number 7 on the map. Building number 8, which is the Jay Memorial Building, is the nearest building east of the fieldhouse.
3. Hancock Building	Find each of the buildings listed by referring to the key. Then use your fingers to measure the walkways to each building, starting each time from the Lee Fine Arts Center. Which trip covered the greatest distance? The Hancock Building is the greatest walking distance from the Lee Fine Arts Center.
4. Eastman Building	Refer to the compass to note directions on the map. Then use the key to find the Administration Building. What building is just south of the Administration Building? The college president sees the Eastman Building when she looks south out of her office in the Administration Building.
5. Yes	Compare the distance between the Hancock Building and Jay Memorial Building with the distance between the Lee Fine Arts Center and Borton Tower. Use your fingers to help compare measurements. The distance to Lorraine's next class appears to be about the distance it takes her 10 minutes to walk. So she can expect to be on time to her next class.
6. Edward	Find the locations of Edward's and Nichole's first and second classes. Use your fingers to measure the distances between classes. Which distance seems further? It appears Edward has the longer walk between classes.

Answers to 5.13.2

Correct Answer	Explanation
1. Study Rooms	Use the compass to find west and then see what is west of the Young Adult Fiction section. The Study Rooms are west of the Young Adult Fiction section.
2. south of the information desk	Refer to the compass to note directions on the map. Find the information desk and the Adult Non-Fiction section on the map. Notice the Adult Non-Fiction section is south of the information desk.
3. No	Look at all the labels on the map. Do you see any restrooms noted? There are no restrooms on this floor of the library.
4. Newspapers	Find the Adult Reference Section and the copy machines on the map. Then trace an imaginary line to the copy machines and notice what you pass. To get to the copy machines from the Adult Reference section, you need to walk past the Newspapers section.
5. near the Study Rooms	First find the Children's Fiction section. Then check to see which of the locations listed are near this area. The Study Rooms are close to the Children's Fiction section.
6. the Adult Audio/Visual (A/V) section	First think about where you would expect to find a video in a library. Most libraries have areas for audiovisual (a/v) materials. Look to see if there is an audiovisual area in this library. Barry should go to the Adult Audio/Visual (A/V) section of the library.

Answers to 5.14.1

Correct Answer	Explanation
1. 13%	Locate the recycling piece and look at the percent. The proportion waste recycled in the U.S. in 1990 was 13%.
2. Incineration	Look for the second largest piece of the pie and read the label. The second most popular method of waste management in 1990 was incineration (14% of the waste).
3. the whole pie represents all waste disposed of in the United States	This is a correct assumption. The pie stands for all waste disposal in 1990.
each piece of the pie shows one method of disposing of waste	This is also true. Each piece shows you how much waste was disposed in a certain way.
all the percents listed add up to 100%	This is a correction assumption. Each pie piece represents a proportion of the whole. All must add up to 100% to get a whole.
4. get smaller	Yes. As one portion of the pie gets larger, the others must get smaller.
5. 3/4	Look at the Landfill piece of the pie. Ask yourself: About what fraction of the whole does this piece look like? It looks like about 3/4 of the pie.
6. got bigger	If the recycling piece of the pie got bigger in future years, this would suggest that efforts to increase recycling were having an effect.

Answers to 5.14.2

Correct Answer	Explanation
1. 17%	Locate the Great Lakes piece of the pie and look at the percent. Seventeen percent of the U.S. coastal population lived on the Great Lakes shoreline in 1991.
2. Southeast	Look for the smallest piece of the pie and read the label. The Southeast had the smallest coastal population in 1991 (8%).
3. 1/4	Find the Pacific Coast part of the pie. About what fraction of the pie is it? It appears to be about 1/4 (or 25%).
4. Gulf of Mexico and Southeast	Find the Great Lakes piece of the pie. Which two other pieces together look about the same size? The pieces for the Gulf of Mexico (13%) and the Southeast (8%) are about the same size as the Great Lakes piece of the pie (17%).
5. 9%	Find the Great Lakes piece of the pie and the Pacific piece. Subtract the % for the Great Lakes region from the % for the Pacific region. The coastal population of the Great Lakes region was 9% less than the coastal population of the Pacific region in 1990.
6. Northeast	Find the largest piece of the pie (the Northeast-- 35%). This is the region the Coast Guard should target first if they want to reach the most coastal dwellers.

Answers to 5.15.1

Correct Answer	Explanation
1. Records	Look for the second largest piece of the 1985 pie. In 1985, records had the second largest percentage of total shipments (44%).
2. CDs	Look for the second largest piece of the 1991 pie. In 1991, CDs had the second largest percentage of total shipments (43%).
3. 3%	Find the *Record* pieces of the 1991 pie. Note the percentage this piece represents (3%).
4. 1/2	Look at the Cassettes piece of the 1991 pie. About what fraction of the pie does this appear to be? It appears to be over 1/2 (or 50%).
5. 40-50%	Look at the 1991 pie. What percent is CDs? (43%) If Jared wants to keep current with the demand for CDs (assuming shipments reflect the demands of consumers), he should have between 40-50% of his inventory in CDs.
6. the CD piece will get bigger than the cassette piece	The information from the magazine seems to suggest that demand for CDs will surpass demand for Cassettes in the future. So you would expect the CD piece of the pie to get bigger than the cassette piece.

Answers to 5.15.2

Correct Answer	Explanation
1. Red meat	Look for the largest piece of the 1989 pie. Red meat was eaten more often than poultry or seafood in 1989.
2. Poultry Seafood	Look for pieces of the pie that were larger in 1989 than in 1971. The average U.S. consumer ate more poultry and seafood in 1989 (the Poultry piece of the pie is much bigger in 1989 than in 1971). The percentage of poultry eaten in 1989 was 32% of the total meat consumed, compared to only 19% in 1971. The seafood increased by only 3% from 1971 to 1989.
3. 1/4	Find the Seafood and Poultry pieces of the 1971 pie. Ask yourself: About what fraction of the pie do these two pieces together make? Seafood and poultry made up 1/4 (or 25%) of the meat consumed in 1971.
4. by about 10%	Look at the percentages listed next to the Poultry pieces of the 1971 and 1989 pies. Subtract these percentages to get the increase in 1989. Poultry consumption increased by about 10% between 1971 and 1989.
5. increase the seafood and poultry recipes	You learned from the pie charts that seafood and poultry consumption increased in 1989. So, Martha should probably increase the seafood and poultry recipes in her book.

6. Yes	Look to see if the Red Meat piece of the pie gets smaller in 1989. The Red Meat piece of the pie is smaller in the 1989 pie than the 1971 pie. Red meat consumption decreased in 1989. So it appears that the health awareness groups were successful.

Answers to 5.16.1

Correct Answer	Explanation
1. D-132	Look across the Ad Copy & Layout row and under the Room column. The Ad Copy & Layout class is in room D-132.
2. 5:30-9:00 a.m.	Look under the Days column for a listing that shows "M" by itself. Then look under the Time column on that same row. Basic Drawing class, section 105-02 is only offered on Mondays from 5:30-9:00 a.m.
3. B. Streep	Look under the Days column for a listing that shows only "T Th." Then look across that row under the Instructor column. The instructor for the Basic Drawing class offered on Tuesday and Thursday is B. Streep.
4. ART 105-02	Look under the Course Title column and find the Basic Drawing class. Look across under the Days column and make sure you have the row for the Basic Drawing class on Mondays (M). Then trace your finger across under the Course Number column and note the number of this class. It is ART 105-02.

5. Basic Drawing	Look down the Cr. Hrs. column until you find 4 listed. Then look across the row to see which course the 4 belongs to. Lan should take basic drawing to get the needed credits.
6. Basic Drawing	Look under the Days and Times columns and eliminate any classes (rows) that conflict with Julia's work times (Wed. and Thurs. noon to 5:00 p.m.). Basic Drawing is the only class that doesn't conflict with Julia's work schedule. She can choose to take either section of this class.

Answers to 5.16.2

Correct Answer	Explanation
1. Tuesday, 3 p.m.	Locate Carol's name on the chart. Then look for the column and row headings. Carol Ong's appointment is on Tuesday at 3 p.m.
2. Monday	Look for the column with the most names listed. Monday is the busiest day. There are four appointments, plus lunch.
3. Wednesday, 1 p.m. and Thursday, 10 a.m.	Use row and column headings to check each appointment. New appointments can be made on Wednesday at 1 p.m. and Thursday at 10 a.m. The other times are already booked.
4. mornings	Count the number of appointments scheduled for the mornings and for the afternoons. There are 4 appointments scheduled for the afternoons and 5 appointments for the mornings.

5. Monday, Wednesday, Friday	Look across the 3 p.m. row to see which other days (excluding Thursday) have open slots. Sandy can reschedule her appointment for either Monday, Wednesday, or Friday.
6. Thursday	Look across the 9:00 a.m. row for openings that are also followed by an opening at 10:00, leaving out Wednesday. Thursday is the only day that has both 9:00 and 10:00 a.m. open.

Answers to 5.17.1

Correct Answer	Explanation
1. Coney St.	Count over four column headings. The fourth bus stop on route #33 is Coney St.
2. 7:14 a.m.	Find the Grayshon Dr. column and locate the third number under that column. It is 7:14 a.m. So, the third bus of the day leaves Grayshon Drive at 7:14 a.m.
3. 11:04 a.m.	Look at the last row in the Foxwood Ave. column. This is the time the last bus reaches Foxwood Ave. (11:04 a.m.).
4. about 30 minutes later	Look under the Main Street column. Then look at the departure times for the first two buses. The first bus leaves at 6:19 a.m. and the second one leaves at 6:47 a.m. If you subtract 19 minutes from 47 minutes, you get 28 minutes. So, the second bus leaves about 30 minutes after the first one.

5. the 8:32 bus	Look under the Coney St. column until you find an arrival time that is at least 30 minutes before 10:00 a.m. It looks like the best arrival time would be 8:41 a.m. because the next time listed is 10:01 a.m. (and that's too late). Next trace across this 8:41 row until your finger is on the departure time under the Main Street heading. It should say 8:32 a.m. So Tameeka should take the 8:32 bus from Main Street to make her 10:00 a.m. appointment near Coney Street.
6. the 7:46 bus	Look under the Foxwood Ave. column and find the latest arrival time before 8:00 a.m. (it is 7:58). Then trace your finger across from this number until you are under the Clifton Rd. column. This shows you that Chester must take the 7:46 bus.

Answers to 5.17.2

Correct Answer	Explanation
1. Folk's the Game	Trace across the 9:00 a.m. row and look under the Wed. column. The program called *Folk's the Game* is on the air at 9 a.m. on Wednesday.
2. 8:00 a.m.	Locate the *Sweet and Blue* cell on the schedule. Then look at the start time for the program that follows *Sweet and Blue*. This is the finish time of *Sweet and Blue*. *Sweet and Blue* finishes at 8 a.m.
3. Breakfast Jam	Look for the program that covers the most time slots (cells) on the schedule. *Breakfast Jam* gets the most air time. It's on every day for two hours (from 7:00 to 9:00 a.m.) Monday through Friday.

4. Radio Venex	Look down the Sunday column and find the program that covers two time slots on the schedule. *Radio Venex* plays for two hours (8:00 to 10:00 a.m.) on Sunday mornings.
5. before 9:00 a.m. or after 10:00 a.m.	Look at the schedule and find when Reggae Runnin' is on (Saturdays, 9:00 to 10:00 a.m.). Howard should tell his friends that he can play basketball before 9:00 a.m. or after 10 a.m. on Saturdays.
6. Yes	Find the times and days of Gisela's classes on the programming schedule. Do any of these times conflict with *Take-2*? None of the times conflict. So Gisela will be able to continue listening to her favorite program.

Answers to 5.18.1

Correct Answer	Explanation
1. Iron	Look down the *Needed For* column and find "red blood cell production." Then look across the row under the *Mineral* column and see what mineral is needed. Iron is needed for red blood cell production.
2. Sources	The foods where minerals are found are discussed under the *Sources* column heading.
3. meat, milk, vegetables	Look across the *Calcium* row and under the *Sources* column. Check to see which foods listed appear in this cell. Meat, milk, and vegetables are all sources of calcium.

4. phosphorus	Look for ATP in one of the descriptions under the Needed For column. When you find it, look across the row and see which mineral is needed to make ATP. Phosphorus is needed to make ATP.
5. calcium, phosphorus	Look under the *Needed For* column and find any places that bones are mentioned. Then look across the row and see which mineral is needed. Calcium and phosphorus are needed for strong bones and teeth.
6. iodine	Look down the *Needed For* column to find the thyroid gland mentioned. Then look across the row at the type of mineral needed.

Answers to 5.18.2

Correct Answer	Explanation
1. $1.55	Look across the price row and under the 1970 column. In 1970, the average admission price to a motion picture theater was $1.55.
2. 1980	Find 1,022 on the chart (remember, numbers are listed in millions). Then look up and notice the column heading. In 1980 the theater attendance was 1,022,000,000.
3. about $1.00	Look across the admission row under the 1970 and 1980 columns. The admission price for 1970 was $1.55 and the price in 1980 was $2.69. There is about a dollar difference in these prices.

4. about 40 million	Compare the attendance numbers under the 1980 and 1990 columns. Notice that in 1980 attendance was 1,022 million and in 1990 it was 1,058 million. If you subtract these numbers, you get 36 million. That's closer to 40 than to 30 million. So the best answer is about 40 million.
5. around $6.75	Compare the prices for 1980 and 1990 and estimate the difference (around $2.00). So, if you add $2.00 to the 1990 price ($4.75), you get around $6.75.
6. 1,094,000,000	Find the movie attendance for 1980 and 1990. The difference between these attendance figures is 36 million. If you add 36 million to 1,058 million, you get 1,094 million.

Glossary

arguments: An argument is a position or a point of view. An author supports an argument by explaining it or providing evidence to demonstrate that it is valid.

assume: To assume something means to take it for granted or to act as if it is true.

assumption: Assumptions are the ideas people accept as true.

bar graph: A bar graph shows information by using bars. You can tell "how much" or "how many" by looking at the length of the bars. Bars of different colors or patterns represent different pieces of information.

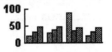

bibliography: A bibliography appears at the end of many books, articles, or research papers. It lists all the written sources, such as books or magazines, that an author has used in writing his or her own work.

catalog: A catalog is a publication that lists different kinds of information, such as the courses a college is offering or the products a store is selling.

chart: A chart is a diagram or drawing that organizes information, often into columns and rows.

clarify: Clarifying means figuring out the meaning of confusing words, sentences, or sections in an article.

column: A column is one way of organizing information in a chart or table. Columns are arranged vertically, that is, in an up-and-down formation.

column

detail: A detail is a specific piece of information on any topic.

drawing on your background knowledge: When you draw on your background knowledge, you think about what you already know and then apply it to the questions you're being asked or the article you're reading.

eliminating answers: When you eliminate answers, you decide that they aren't correct and then ignore them or even cross them out, when possible.

evidence: Evidence is information used by an author to support an argument. Authors use evidence to persuade readers of the validity of their arguments.

examples: Examples are a type of evidence. They are specific things or ideas that illustrate an author's position.

facts: Facts are a type of evidence. They are things that can be seen or observed. Statements of fact aren't necessarily true; but they can be verified or disproved.

heading: A heading is a way of labeling different sections of an article, chart, or other document. A heading usually tells you what a particular section is about.

idea map: An idea map is one way of organizing the most important ideas from an article or research project. Idea maps use boxes, lines, and sometimes colors to show how ideas are connected.

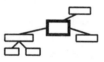

imply: To imply something means to suggest that it is true. When authors imply something, they don't directly state it — they say it *indirectly.*

infer: To infer something means to figure out what is being implied. Sometimes ideas aren't directly stated in an article or other document. You have to figure out what the text *indirectly* says. This is called making an inference or inferring an answer.

inference: An inference is the idea that you come up with when you infer an author's meaning. To make an inference, you figure out what an article or other document *indirectly* says — what it implies.

key: A key tells you what the symbols or colors on a map, chart, or graph represent. For example, a picture of a tent might stand for a camping area.

key
▨ favor
▨ oppose

legend: A legend tells you what the symbols or colors on a map, chart, or graph represent. For example, the yellow sections of a map might stand for the heavily populated areas of a city.

line graph: A line graph uses lines to compare different pieces of information. Each line represents a piece of information.

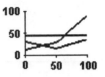

map: A map gives a picture of a place (city, nation, solar system) and provides information about it. Maps can also be created to represent ideas.

most important idea: The most important idea is the main message that a piece of writing expresses — the one idea that ties together all the ideas you have read. The most important idea is sometimes called the main point or main idea.

opinions: Opinions are statements that cannot be verified or disproved, but that may make sense to you.

outline: An outline is one way of organizing the most important ideas from an article or research project. An outline contains brief statements of the author's main message and the ideas that support it.

pie chart: Pie charts show how parts of a whole relate to each other. Each piece of the pie represents a different piece of information.

position: The author's position is the stand he or she takes on a topic. In most cases, the author's position will be an opinion about the way things are or how they ought to be. In a piece of persuasive writing, all the ideas work together to prove or support the author's position.

predicting: Predicting means using what you already know or have read in an article to guess what will happen next.

prediction: A prediction is a guess you make about something you haven't read yet. Making predictions helps you stay focused while you read.

previewing: Previewing means looking at something in advance. For example, you might look at questions before you read an article.

purpose: A purpose is your reason for reading an article or for doing research on a topic.

questioning: Questioning means asking yourself (or fellow students) questions about what you are reading in order to practice finding important ideas.

quotes: Quotes are a type of evidence. They are statements from people who have knowledge or experience, or they may be information from other publications that an author has read.

row: A row is one way of organizing information in a chart or table. Rows are arranged horizontally, that is, in a side-to-side formation.

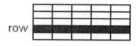

schedule: A schedule tells when and where planned events or activities will take place.

skimming: Skimming means glancing through an article or book to see what it is about.

source: A source is a book or article that you read for a research project.

subtitle: A subtitle follows the title of an article, chart, or other document. Usually, subtitles provide more detail to let you know what the text will be about.

summarizing: Summarizing is a strategy in which you restate in a shortened form what you've read or learned in a shortened form, keeping only the most important ideas. You can summarize any piece of writing: a sentence, a paragraph, a section of text, an article, or an entire book.

summary: A summary is a shortened version of a piece of writing that contains its most important ideas. You can also write a summary of your research to show the most important ideas you have learned.

table: A table organizes information into columns and rows.

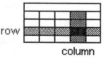

title: A title is given at the beginning of most articles, charts, and other documents. Titles give you a general idea of what a text is about.

topic: A topic is a general idea that you are reading about or researching. It is the subject of an article, chart, or other document.

Index

LearningPlus®

The Handbook Series

The LearningPlus® Handbooks help you develop the skills you need throughout college and beyond.

Student Pack	(1 Reading, 1 Writing, and 1 Mathematics Handbook) priced at $36.00, a $4.00 savings per book.
Individual	Reading, Writing, and Mathematics Handbooks priced at $16.00 each.

LearningPlus® Publication Order Form

ITEM	NUMBER	PRICE	QUANTITY	TOTAL PRICE
Student Pack (3 books)	271561	36.00		
Reading Handbook	274217	16.00		
Writing Handbook	274215	16.00		
Mathematics Handbook	274227	16.00		

If paying by credit card, write in credit card number, expiration date, and type. Do not leave any spaces between the numbers. Only VISA or MasterCard will be accepted.

TOTAL
(Shipping and handling included.)

TYPE OF CREDIT CARD	EXPIRATION DATE		CREDIT CARD NUMBER
☐ VISA	Month	Year	
☐ MasterCard			

Signature _____ Date _____

Send to:

Name _____

Address _____

City _____

State _____ Zip _____

Telephone _____

Payment must be included!

Make checks payable to LearningPlus® and mail to:
LearningPlus
33 S. Delaware Ave.
Suite 202
Yardley, PA 19067